NEW
AGAIN

find your renewal in daily growth.
Andy

Andy Leigh Ptacek

For my sons,

Tavin and Grant.

If you ever feel less than,
just look through my eyes.

CONTENTS

INTRODUCTION

You forget how to breathe or speak. Your heart tries to exit your body through your mouth. Consciousness is relative in this moment. Everything is in slow motion, but you can't actually process any of it.

That is what it feels like when you've been told you're going to die. I know firsthand.

There is fear, of course, but my fear in that moment wasn't about experiencing death; I was afraid to leave my family to a future that I would not be part of.

I was afraid their memory of me would fade to nothing. That the two little humans whom I had grown in my own body would grow up to be adults without any tangible piece of me to help them navigate life. That the man whose soul was so intertwined with mine would be left broken when my half departed.

I wasn't about to leave a mess like that. My will to survive became primal. Everything that mattered became my why. Everything that didn't matter became insignificant. It was all very clear. If there's one thing a death sentence is good for, it's perspective.

God was there. I saw how He'd been working up to this moment as I tried to guess His next move. He equally comforted and angered me.

Had that doctor with the big curly hair just said "brain cancer?" Had that other doctor standing next to her just wiped a freaking tear as if to say a final goodbye before we'd ever properly met?!

What thirty-two-year-old knows how to die? I'm in better shape than ever. I'm running a successful business. My family has barely made it past the starting line!

But this is really happening.

I need to cry hard. Then I need to plan a war.

This book is not about fighting cancer. It's about fighting a battle we all share: the battle to find perspective when we start to spiral. The battle to find intention when we suddenly realize we've been living on autopilot. The battle to live a purposeful life when this world wants to trap us into believing that we are victims of circumstance.

In the thick of it, I couldn't figure out how to be *me* again, because everything was so different.

Then it hit me. *I* was different. I would never be *me* again.

But that is not a curse. It is a privilege that I get to experience every single morning I open my eyes— with a *new* appreciation for the *new* life waiting for me. This is the perspective I had to learn the hard way, but it is also the perspective that healed me from the inside out.

1. MY BROKEN HEART

Adversity happens for us, not to us.

It all started with a broken heart, literally. The kids were finally asleep, and my husband, Bruce, had just served me a bowl of mint chocolate-chip ice cream on the couch while I surfed the TV for something we could wind down to.

A few bites in, my heart started jumping around in my chest. I coughed to try and settle myself, but it didn't stop. Bruce wasn't too concerned. Mind you, he's only slightly jaded from working at a busy firehouse. I honestly don't know how he does it. Most of the time he comes home from a busy shift feeling more like a life coach or hospital shuttle service than a firefighter.

The pounding in my chest gave me the strange urge to go for a run, and I started feeling anxious within the confining walls of our house. "Mind over matter," I kept telling myself. "You are in charge." Consequently, I was halfway through a book on mental toughness for athletes—a concept I was interested in not only for the athletes I coach, but for myself. I always felt like my mind would give up before I gave my body a chance to see what it was capable of. The tactics I was learning were helping me lean on my mind versus the natural response to freak out. I believe the technical term for this type of freak-out would be considered "fight or flight."

I kept bringing my spiraling mind back to the facts. *I am not in pain. I am standing right here. I am moving on my own will. I can breathe.*

I calmly stepped out of my clothes and into a warm shower to coax my body into relaxing and my jumping-bean heart into following suit.

It wasn't working.

Okay, I'm actually freaking out now.

Do you know the *Seinfeld* episode where the high-strung character Frank Costanza is advised to say "serenity now" to suppress his emotions and stay calm? It's a classic, and you'll be immediate best friends with my entire family if you can relate to *Seinfeld* humor. Anyway, remember how well that worked for Frank and everyone else? Serenity now—insanity later! That was literally happening to me, but it didn't take a whole half-hour episode to unfold. In less than ten minutes I went from calm and in control to ugly crying in the shower, fully expecting "the big one" to take me out any second.

Bless Bruce's heart for dealing with my crazy all these years. I mean, I know this situation had the potential to be serious, but this swing of emotions is pretty much my MO, and he's become a master at knowing when to let me cry it out or when to tell me to grow a spine and stand up.

But this was one of those rare times when he was walking the line—not sure which approach to take.

With dripping-wet hair and red eyes, I sat on the bed and pulled my arm out of my bathrobe as he grabbed his stethoscope from the nightstand. He tried to read my pulse, but it was so irregular he couldn't make sense of it. By now my hands and feet were cold and tingling.

Bruce did the most natural thing he could think of in this moment—he called his captain paramedic for advice. Hugh is an epic problem solver. If his huge biceps fool you, his classic nerdy black glasses will set the record straight.

He and Bruce said some big words back and forth, and when they hung up, Bruce told me we needed to get checked out at the hospital.

Okay, we have a plan. I love a plan. I can work with a plan. Goal: Don't die on the way to the hospital.

Yes, I was super dramatic. This was my first adult health scare, and I had recently entered the ripe old age of thirty-two so I figured it was all downhill from here. No longer would I be CrossFitting and weightlifting; I would be pulling around an oxygen tank and giant pill organizer and I'd probably grow a hunch-back, because why not?! Based solely on the events of tonight, I could see it all unfolding in my mind as we drove to the small neighborhood hospital only a couple miles down the road. Just enough time to let my imagination spiral.

When we arrived at the emergency room we were taken back immediately (pro tip—heart stuff gets you to the front of the line). Before I knew it I had all kinds of leads on my chest, but everyone relaxed when the doc told me I was in classic AFib, or atrial fibrillation. According to my mom, AFib runs in my dad's side of the family. I had no idea because he's been MIA since the summer of sixth grade. More on that later.

While AFib is pretty treatable and not life-threatening, I *would* have to lay off high-intensity workouts for a little bit. Dagger to the heart! Might as well kill me now!

To put things in perspective, I was never the girl who liked to work out. When my softball or cheer coaches would make us work out I hated every second of it because it felt like punishment. It wasn't until I had my first son that I actually tried to nurture my body and take care of it. It felt so good to accomplish goals like getting my first pull-up or seeing my body morph into something even stronger than I ever thought possible for myself. Working out gave me a sense of control over my body while simultaneously releasing all the stresses of being a new mom and business owner. It had become *my thing*. Don't take away *my thing*!

While I was contemplating my torturous future without barbells or box jumps, the doc gave me some meds and said they should bring down my heart rate and hopefully bring it back to normal sinus rhythm. If not, they'd just shock me back to normal.

Um, *excuse* me?

Bruce perked up as if it was his lifelong dream to see someone—his wife, no less—get jolted with a crap ton of electricity.

Maybe it was Bruce's reaction or maybe it was seeing the nurse roll in the giant heart-shocking machine "just in case," but my heart started beating so rapidly—because of, I don't know, *fear*—that it somehow found its way back to a normal rhythm. Thank you, Jesus.

The routine heart ablation and short-term meds didn't seem so bad after all.

2. WHAT THE HELL

Setbacks are often setups.

The procedure was successful. As I woke up, Bruce was nowhere to be found. I sat in my room, staring at the white wall in front of me, noticing all the weird pains. My throat especially hurt from the breathing tube, but I was instructed not to cough, since the procedure was initiated from my groin. Ugh, that hurt too.

He eventually came walking into my room with a goofy smile, holding a cafeteria cup, and my first words to him were, "What the hell?!"

Why wasn't he sitting with bated breath in one of those uncomfortable little waiting room chairs for the past few hours, anxiously waiting for me to emerge? He'd totally ditched me! Did he not care for me at all? Who did he think he was, to walk into my room post-op with his freaking cafeteria cup, all smiles and jerk-faced? I'd just had *heart surgery*, and he was gallivanting downstairs in the cafeteria!

Okay, so remember in the last chapter how I mentioned it was a routine surgery? It really was. They cut a tiny hole in my groin area and fed an instrument through an artery up to my heart to do their thing. But to be fair, I hadn't been hospitalized since having kids, so I was totally projecting my fears onto Bruce. His face dropped from all smiles to that deer-in-the-headlights look husbands get. He walked over, sat his stupid cafeteria cup down on my tray, looked me in the eyes, and calmed my crazy. When he kissed my head I immediately forgave him for existing.

And to set the record straight, *anesthesia* is crazy. *I* wasn't crazy—yet.

~~~

Soon enough I was easing back into workouts with a heart monitor. Of course, it wasn't a discrete one. I looked like I was wearing a Walkman with way too many headphones. As an introvert, I was pretty mortified. People were going to look at me and want to talk about my bum heart. I felt embarrassed. I was supposed to be a healthy role model to the hundreds of people I coached at our gym, CrossFit Incendia, but here I was with a weak heart, when we work our tails off to have strong ones.

Believe me, I know how irrational this sounds, but I believe every kind of growth starts with an irrational thought. We have to start by articulating why we feel like we do, and most of the time, when we investigate that irrational thought logic reels us back in and helps us start to form a new, enlightened perspective based on what we know and have learned. This relatively small adversity, in retrospect, was the beginning of that for me.

~~~

My new morning routine started by reaching over for a device to test my resting heart rate before I sat up. I did this faithfully and was encouraged by steady improvement. I was finally waking up with beats per minute in the sixties instead of the nineties. All that rule-following, with the gaudy heart monitor and keeping my workouts moderately paced, was paying off. I was doing it!

Then bam, my first migraine.

Of course Bruce was on shift. It's a cosmic rule that every public-safety wife knows to be true. All the big things happen when you're alone to fend for yourself.

Before I get into my own experience, I can't go without recognizing anyone reading this who experiences migraines regularly. I admire your strength.

It was the most excruciating pain I had experienced since birthing two large-headed humans into the world. My vision was altered, every noise was ear-piercing, and my stomach was turning with nausea. Meanwhile, my three- and six-year-old boys were acting a fool like mom was just dandy, so I called in reinforcements (my mom).

After just a few minutes with me, she called in her own reinforcements (Bruce's mom) to come watch the kids so she could take me back to the same neighborhood hospital where I'd had my ablation. She was afraid I might be having a complication from the procedure.

We were walking toward the emergency room entrance when I stopped, grabbed my mom's arm, and made her take me home.

"I am not going to be one of those people that Bruce tells me about after a long shift—the people who think knee pain and diarrhea are emergencies. I am not going to the hospital for a headache."

She reluctantly took me home, but it got worse. This must have sent her mom instincts into full force, because she started using every mom's secret weapon: fear tactics. She scared me straight with the small, tiny, minute chance that the migraine could have something to do with a blood clot that could have left my healing heart and landed in my brain. So I gave in, really without any wherewithal to resist, and we went back.

As much as I felt in control over my health after all the hard work and discipline *I* had accomplished to get *my* heart back on track, I was suddenly out of control again. I had never felt pain like this, and what happened next wasn't up to me at all.

The nurse gave me a wonder drug, and my headache disappeared almost instantly. Then I was asked to follow a series of commands, passing the "stroke test." But just to rule everything out, I needed to also pass a precautionary brain scan before I went home.

3. LET THERE BE LIGHT

Don't ignore that little voice, that gut feeling, your intuition—they could be nudges from God to step onto a new path.

Something was glowing on the brain scans. I had no idea what this meant, but I got the sense that it was serious by the way the nurse who had been cheerfully helping me was anxiously shadowing the doctor as he delivered the news.

"We're not sure what it is, but it's something. It might be a stroke, but I'll have to bring in a neurologist on this to decide the next steps."

I was confused because I had no deficits. In fact, I felt freaking amazing after the magic migraine drug.

When they left the room, my mom and I stared at each other with big, bulging eyes. What the heck had just happened? For clarity and a sound voice of reason, I called the ever-steady Bruce.

Without question, he came straight over from the fire station, still in uniform. Being the introverted people pleaser I am wired to be, I hated being the one to interrupt everyone's day, especially when I felt completely fine now. Surely the doctor or the imaging tech had gotten it wrong.

I'm fine. Everything's fine.

But it wasn't fine. I was admitted to the hospital to begin solving whatever this little light was telling us.

By now, it had been hours since the scan, but no one was *doing* anything. I found out that I wouldn't be able to talk to another neurologist until tomorrow. The neurologist I had spoken with today was over an online video call. Would tomorrow's neurologist be able to examine me in person and make sense of my scans?

Frustrated, I remembered my mother-in-law was still holding it down with the kids. I realize most women have a complicated relationship with their mother-in-law, but mine is a saint. For real. She's made-me-eggs-on-my-walk-of-shame-the-second-time-I-met-her kind of sainthood. She's let-us-live-in-a-trailer-in-her-backyard-for-a-year-while-we-get-our-crap-together kind of sainthood. Told you.

While she was keeping it together with the kids, I was starting to unravel in a now-dark hospital room. This was taking too long. If it was truly a stroke they saw on the scan, there was a small window of opportunity in which to avoid long-term effects. A fire started growing in my gut as I realized I was trapped in a place that could not help me. I wanted to leave. Now.

Bruce, being the "fixer" he is and not really knowing what to do, called Hugh again. Hugh was always very careful with his words and had perfected the tightrope walk between my innate earnestness and Bruce's reactive hesitation over the years. If anyone had a sober mind in the moment it was him.

I sat there crisscross-legged on the bed, lines coming out of everywhere, staring at Bruce's every facial expression, trying to clue together where the conversation was going. It didn't take long to realize Hugh was on my level of urgency. When Bruce hung up, we agreed that it was time to leave, but that was "against medical advice," which basically means against the rules.

Going against my natural people-pleasing tendencies, I pressed the nurse's button. My whole body wanted out of that room. When she arrived I told her our plan to go to a different hospital, but she was pulling out all the stops on why we needed to stay. So I did, too, on all the reasons I needed to leave.

Before long it turned into pleading, then ugly crying. At that she agreed to let me talk to the on-call doctor over the phone. He also disagreed with my decision, but all this resistance was just fanning the flames. Tears kept rolling down my face, but my attitude changed from polite to willful.

My life and wellbeing was *not* theirs to dictate. It was not up to them. It was up to *me*. So I told the nurse, "I'm leaving," and ripped off that too-tight finger monitor while Bruce helped me peel off the heart-monitor leads. The room filled with loud beeps and alarms as if I was dying right then and there. But I wasn't dying; I was *standing*. I was standing up for myself in pink hospital socks on the cold floor.

The nurse rushed over to turn off the loud monitors and just as quickly left to bring back paperwork that basically said I'd be receiving a swift kick to my bank account for leaving. But money meant nothing at a time like this. I signed all the papers and handed the clipboard back to her as I walked out.

When we stepped into the elevator and the door closed, I couldn't believe I had just done that. But I knew it was right, and I knew that feeling inside me was right. My kids were all I could think about. I needed to be able to hold them. To talk to them. To raise them properly. How could I do that if this apparent blood clot in my brain took me down? What would happen to them? To Bruce? He couldn't take care of all of us. I had to get to the bottom of this.

Hugh had already called ahead to a friend at a more equipped city hospital, and they were waiting for us when we got there.

4. TELL ME SOMETHING

The most important things in life happen in the details.

"It's not a stroke, but it's not normal. We'll need to admit you for further tests."

I breathed a sigh of relief. Whatever it was couldn't be that bad. I was in the best shape of my life, and I ate particularly healthily, with the exception of my fine dark-chocolate addiction (the other stuff just isn't even worth it. Besides, I hadn't even had so much as a cold in ages. As far as I could see, this was *good* news. I hadn't stroked out!

It was nearly morning by the time we got sorted and moved into our room. Our parents tag-teamed the kids, which was clutch, but not unusual. They have a history of coming through for us. One day I want to be just like them, on so many levels.

My in-laws raised two boys, just like us. God bless them, because it's tough. They've shown me it's possible to turn rowdy, emotional, physical, dirty little boys into good men. Men like my husband are not what I grew up with. He is equal parts kindhearted and strong, thanks to his mom and dad.

But my mom had to assume the role of both mother and father for most of my life. Watching her do the hard things like work two jobs, put herself through school, and push a freaking lawn mower only to get up every day and do it again is the reason I'm strong enough to get vulnerable and write this book. She always made me believe I could do whatever I was daring enough to attempt.

~~~

When I was a little girl, in my signature ponytail, tank top, and Levi's, my mom gifted me with my first big-girl bike—and told me to ride it. No helmet, no pads; this was old-school do-or-die kid life. Sure, I fell a few times, but I *learned* and I *achieved*.

Then there was high school softball, when I was pulled off my starting position at third base to play catcher for our injured backup. I had only practiced the position a handful of times before that day, but it was time to "put on my big-girl panties," like Coach Prado would say, and step up to the plate. A freak pitch nailed my thumb and broke the knuckle. The athletic trainer came over and taped a splint on it. My mom was standing by watching, and when I was all taped up, she told me to shove it in my glove and get back out there. So I did. Every pitch hurt. Every pitch made me stronger.

Then as an adult, pregnant and finally using my college degree, working for a PR agency, I decided

I couldn't spend another day in rush-hour traffic, climbing (clawing is probably a more appropriate word) my way to the top of a ladder with broken steps. I told her that I wanted to quit my job and that I also wanted her boyfriend, who moonlighted as a freelance web designer, to also quit his job, so we could start our own business.

Let's just put this into perspective for a second. Her second marriage had fizzled, and after years of dating jerks she *finally* had a promising boyfriend, and I wanted him to quit his well-paying and steady job to go into business with me, her daughter, in the middle of the 2008 recession. Crazy, right?

Well, she told me that if I could line up three contracts she would be on board with our big dream. Guess who lined up three contracts in less than thirty days? She shook her head with a smile and maybe disbelief. She told us to go for it. Now here we are, well over a decade later, still bringing in those contracts.

She was a single mom, and my grammie was a single mom; thus, I was raised with a little extra grit—a trait I am eternally grateful for. Taking on whatever this medical scare would turn out to be was what I was *raised* to do. I knew that I could overcome it and that my mom would be my biggest advocate, next to my husband.

~~~

But we still didn't know what we were dealing with. Test after test, scan after scan, I had never been poked and prodded like this in my life: bloodwork (ouch!), echocardiogram (basically an ultrasound of the heart), bubble study (shoving bubbles into my heart through an IV and watching on the ultrasound to see if everything was flowing correctly), CT (computerized tomography) scans with and without IV contrast dye, MRI (magnetic resonance imaging) scans with and without IV contrast dye, and—one that should have piqued my interest—a PET (positron emission tomography) scan. And all in one day!

But can we just pause for a moment and get real about something? I was still extremely claustrophobic. Do you know how they take brain scans? You lie on a hard table, with your feet propped up so they don't fall asleep, then the technician slides you into an extremely loud, tiny tube for eternity. You can't even see out of the tube, because your knees are in the way. If at any moment you stop clutching your hands together tightly over the top of your body, your arms will touch the sides of the tiny tube, and you'll actually *feel* how small it is. I almost forgot the kicker—the face cage. I don't know if there's a technical term for it, but I call it like it is. It's a cage that slides over your face and locks your head to the table. It's a face cage. It's also stuffed with foam to make extra sure you can't move.

At this point I was so exhausted that I complied to it all without asking a lot of questions—but I did make sure to ask for something to help me relax every time they wanted to put me back in the tiny tube.

After the entire medical staff in the hospital got to play with all their fancy toys in the pursuit of exacting my diagnosis, I finally got to see my kids.

They were accompanied by my mom; my stepdad, Brad; and my little brother, Chase. I remember Grant, my youngest, who was three at the time, walked in very cautiously with big, full eyes. Tavin, my oldest, who was six, was trying to be tough for his brother, although I know how freaked out he must have been. On more than one occasion we've had to calm him down after walking in on us watching *Grey's Anatomy*. This was sensory overload for both of them.

To calm their little nerves I pulled a latex glove from a box on the wall, blew it up like a balloon, and hit it into the air. Everyone joined in the volley, trying to keep it from touching the floor. Everything was slow motion for me. Life was moving as slow as that hand balloon, floating from one person to the next. I looked at everyone's faces. Everyone was smiling and belting out uncontrollable laughter when there was a clumsy miss. Life was simple for a moment, and we had all forgotten about this dark cloud about to drown us.

5. A DEATH SENTENCE

Intentionally acknowledge the battles of others before it comes full circle.

Earlier that day I had texted my best friend, Julia, who was coincidentally a trauma nurse at the same hospital. It just so happened she was working that day. She had promised to break away at some point to see me because she could tell I was anxious. I think the words I used were along the lines of "I'm starting to go crazy . . . I might as well be in a psych ward . . . now I know what test bunnies feel like . . . all the plants are fake . . . they can't even keep plants alive here." I love being dramatic with her.

My brother and Brad had just left to take the boys home when Steve, my mom's second husband, who saw me grow up from about sixth grade to college, had stopped by to be with us while we waited for news. Bruce's parents were right behind him.

They walked in flustered and a little out of breath. Come to find out, their elevator had gotten stuck on the way up to the room. We recalled the recent commotion over the intercom about "the elevator situation" but had never imagined it could be *them*! We all busted up laughing over the odds and the irony, carrying on into lighthearted conversation in the small hospital room. Everyone was curious to know what all the test results would conclude, but we didn't really talk about it. The whole day was a lot of hurry up and wait, until it wasn't.

The head neurologist walked in.

I could feel the energy drop to the floor, right next to the deflated latex glove from our game earlier. She was a tall, curly-haired lady, and she didn't come alone. The other five or so white coats accompanying her were young and apprehensive. I believe it was a teaching moment for them, on how to give a horrible diagnosis.

My heart was pounding so loudly I could barely hear her words, but what I *could* hear wasn't making any sense. She was being very professional and using medical terms I wasn't familiar with. I finally heard the word *tumor*. Okay, I could handle a tumor. We could handle a tumor. *It's probably not, but I have to ask her anyway.*

"Is it cancer?"

I fully expected her to say no, but she looked me dead in the face and nodded her head yes. The silence that followed was physically painful.

I sank heavily into the hospital bed—inside out—trying to process what I was just told. The first thing that made sense was the thought of my kids.

"Am I going to live long enough to raise my kids?"

Another long pause.

When I saw one of the young doctors standing toward the back wipe her face, it became clear to me that a long life was unlikely.

I could feel the heat coming off Bruce, who was sitting next to me on the hospital bed, and my heart broke for him.

The curly-haired neurologist said some more doctor-y things and let me know that a neurosurgeon would pay me a visit next to discuss our options.

In hindsight, I know now that statistics are *not* a God thing. Let me say that again in case you or someone you love is going through something they are not "likely" to make it out of: statistics are *not* a God thing. But when this news was hitting me for the first time, it felt like a death sentence. When the doctors left the room, they took our future with them.

Before anyone said a word, I asked my family to give me a moment alone. Without question they quickly filed out of the room. It seemed as though everyone was holding their breath, their emotions, or both. I know I was. When the door shut behind them, Bruce and I made eye contact for the first time since hearing the words *brain cancer*.

"I'm sorry," I told him.

He barely let me finish before he pulled me into his chest, and we both just fell apart in uncontrollable tears. Time stopped for us in this moment as we released every bit of tension that had been building up over the last couple days.

Then we stopped, like we both had the same thought at the same time—*we are going to fight to win.* And that was that. Making that choice together gave us our power back.

This response to the diagnosis was a choice that I had to make not just in this moment, but over and over again whenever doubt crept in. I had to choose it now and in the years ahead until it became my truth, until it was engraved on my heart. I believe that when you choose something with all your heart, your heart opens your mind to possibilities that support your choice. An open heart and a mind that has direction can ultimately nurture ideas and actions that have the power to influence the future. I didn't know that yet, but I was already nurturing a future that was starting to take shape with that one response, that one choice. To fight.

With a deep breath and brave smiles, we wiped our tears, and Bruce left to see our family members to their cars. I didn't want to be alone in that moment, so I sent Julia another text and called Cidney, my high school friend through thick and thin. She's one of those enchanting deep thinkers who are somehow simultaneously grounded. She knows my heart, and I needed someone outside those hospital walls to confide in—like, now.

She picked up right away, and my gut instantly twisted as I tried to find my words. Eventually I said the *C* word, out loud, for the very first time. My voice cracked, and in the silence I could hear her tears too. I told her not to cry, that it was going to be okay, but we both cried anyway. She didn't want to talk about any medical stuff, just the important stuff... like whether or not we'd still take our trip to Disneyland with the boys and how lucky I was that the boys were getting old enough to form some really solid memories about me if I didn't make it.

"You know, you've got more time with your kids than some people get," she said to me. This was the honest-to-God perspective I needed, as morbid as it might sound. "So much of you is already instilled in them. You've shaped them more than you realize into who they are and who they are going to be, regardless of their age."

I was choosing to believe all of this, but I had to say something out loud that I'd never really admitted before.

"I've always had a feeling I wouldn't make it to see them grow up. I don't know why, but I've never been able to imagine that far into the future. In fact, I've been keeping journals for them on the off chance something like this would happen..."

I knew she wouldn't judge me for saying that, even though *I know* it can be taken a thousand different wrong ways. Instead, she helped me find peace in that. The whole conversation calmed my nerves and cleansed my soul.

"I'm going to fight like hell, but if I'm not meant to make it," I said, "I sure will leave them with an amazing dad."

She agreed, and we left it at that. It was exactly the honest conversation I needed at that moment.

We had no sooner hung up than Julia walked into my room, wearing crisp scrubs from work and a smile. I was sitting crisscross on my bed, and she was sitting to my left in a small plastic chair. She was on her game. She kept that smile going, all the way up until I said "cancer." She tried her damnedest to keep that smile, but her eyes welled up and gave her strong facade away.

Julia had lost her mom earlier that year to lung cancer that had metastasized to her brain. It was the brain cancer that killed her. Now here I was, telling her I had it too.

I don't know where the tears were coming from at this point, but I cried again with her as we talked. I realized I was opening up a fresh wound, intensely regretting that I hadn't been there for her the way she was here for me right now. Julia is one of the most independent people I know, and I had mostly let her keep to herself in that time because I assumed it was her way of healing. I assumed that would be my way of healing too, but it clearly wasn't. Bruce had been gone approximately forty-five minutes at this point, and I'd already had deep conversations that were more healing than I could have ever experienced solo. I should have pushed my way into her grief. I will always live with that regret. I didn't understand this beast or the real sting of death.

Bruce finally returned after seeing off various family members who had wandered around the hospital to process the news in their own ways in hallways, lobbies, and parking garages. It had been a long day for everyone, and Bruce would spend another night in a hospital-room recliner.

The next morning we got our long-awaited visit from the neurosurgeon. *Okay, here we go.* I prepared myself to hear some gnarly plan of attack about brain-surgery tactics. *He's going to tell us how we can beat this thing.*

"Your tumor is inoperable."

Wait, what?

Any hope I had was getting dimmer with each word he said after that. I was surprised how easily and quickly my mind went to the dark place. That choosing-to-fight-and-win conviction was so flimsy it was already wearing off. I started to imagine how sick I might get and how long I would be lucid before I wasn't really me anymore and how long my family would have to see me like that before I died. This scared me, but not because I would experience it. It scared me because my family would, and I couldn't protect them from that. Had I lived well enough up to this point to give them clear and beautiful memories of me before I got sick, or would they always remember the frail, mindless body that withered away to death?

I snapped back just in time to catch the neurosurgeon's plan. He wanted to drill a hole in my skull to biopsy the tumor and formulate the best treatment plan from there. I was numb but on board. All I really knew was that I needed a hospital break.

6. SMILE ANYWAY

Surrender is a decision to hope.

As a fitness coach, I always tell my athletes to smile when they're in pain. It takes so much more energy to grimace and tense up than it does to just relax your face and smile. It also tells your brain to tell your body that it can keep enduring the pain. I remembered this as I navigated the aftermath of my diagnosis. I didn't feel like smiling, cooped up in that hospital, but I did anyway. It helped knowing that although the doctors thought they were in control of my treatment plan, I had plans of my own.

Protocol was to keep me in the hospital to proceed with a biopsy that would determine the recipe of chemo and radiation treatment, but we had a family vacation scheduled in just a couple of weeks, and I wouldn't miss this opportunity to make *good* memories that would hopefully outweigh the bad ones that lay ahead.

I wasn't sure I could persuade the doctors to let me go, but I harnessed every positive vibe left in me and presented my request. This felt like a Make-A-Wish situation, because the doctor in charge eventually obliged with a reluctance that felt like he was largely bending the rules. By the next shift change, I was already discharged, with instructions to schedule a biopsy as soon as I returned. I'd never packed so fast in my life. I had done my part here with the utmost alacrity, but if I had to spend any more time in that hospital room, I'd surely end up stabbing someone in the forehead with a fork. (Another *Seinfeld* reference.)

The car ride home was surreal. Everything in the outside world looked different. I was imagining all the people walking down the street, sitting at the bus stop or in their cars, with expiration dates they didn't even know about. I had been walking around with one this whole time and hadn't realized it was running out. All this time I thought that I knew death, that I was content with it. I was wrong. Death is freaking scary.

My mind was wrestling with these thoughts, and my body was under attack by cancer, but I was still here, and I was going to put on a smile for my kids when I walked through that door, because they were going to be excited to have their mom back, and I'd be damned if the last thing they learned from me was how to curl up and give up.

~~~

In the weeks leading up to our California trip, I left numerous messages to schedule my biopsy, with no reply. I was blindly going through the motions of what I was told to do, not even thinking beyond whatever was right in front of me. Everything I had known about my life and my future had been yanked from me, shaken up, thrown up in the air and had landed scattered in all the wrong places.

I was so overwhelmed that I just let everything happen to me. I think I was too close to look at the overall magnitude of the situation. Instead, I chose to focus my energy on prayer and being present in the moments I had now, before life got even more unpredictable.

Thankfully, my mom chose to strategize while I was off in la-la land.

"Andy, think about it."

Here she was with her daily call.

"I want you to get a second opinion."

I didn't want to see another doctor.

"I've done some research."

Of course she has.

"And everything points to this amazing neurosurgeon right here in Phoenix."

I thought to myself, *Aren't* all *neurosurgeons amazing?*

She went on to tell me that she had already talked with a nice lady at this surgeon's office, who had promised that if we brought my scans in before lunch, the neurosurgeon would call me by the end of the day.

"Mom, this sounds like a long shot."

She was so persistent.

"Well, I can't get your scans without you, so I'll be over in ten minutes to pick you up."

I mostly got in the car because there was this delicious fruit-infused water in the coffee shop at the hospital where my scans had been taken. I wasn't particularly interested in bringing more people, especially doctors, into the decisions of my life, though.

On the way there I came around to the idea that it did make sense to get a second opinion on such a big diagnosis. When we arrived, I got myself that fancy water and headed over to the records desk, expecting a lot of red tape having just ordered my records on the way over.

"Name?" the lady behind the counter asked me with a blank stare.

"Andy—I mean, Andrea Ptacek." Of course I had to spell it. Did you know my maiden name was Campbell? Everyone got it right. Now people can hardly understand which letters I'm saying in which order. It's the random *C* that always gets them, sitting oddly between an *A* and a *K*.

The amount of time it took her to get my name typed in correctly was definitely not an indicator of how hard it would be to get my records. As soon as she found me, she rolled over to the counter behind her, filed through a couple manila envelopes, and rolled back with mine.

"Here you go. Have a nice day."

That's it? I was starting to think maybe this was meant to be.

When we got back to the car, I opened up the big manila envelope, and we looked at it. I found a page that detailed the size of the tumor, and curiosity got the best of us. We used our fingers to approximate and visualize the measurements. Holding my hands up, I couldn't believe how much of my brain had been taken over. I know now that so many people have survived surgeries to remove much larger brain tumors, but I didn't want to give up *any* of my brain.

Realizing we were getting caught up in all the information now scattered across the front seat, my mom helped me get everything back in order and back in the envelope. She drove us straight to Barrow Neurological Institute at St. Joseph's Hospital, where someone was hopefully expecting us.

That nice lady whom my mom had talked to on the phone was named Rima. I wasn't sure that she'd really be there or that this was really happening, a big-time neurosurgeon taking time to look at *my* scans. I was just a regular person. I was not famous. I didn't have a ton of money to donate to research. I was just lost. Rima knew the road well, and she knew if anyone could operate on an "inoperable" tumor, it would be Dr. Sanai.

I saw her walking toward us, all smiles. She was a petite, shiny angel who was really real. She took the large manila envelope and matter-of-factly told me to expect a call from Dr. Sanai later that day. I wanted to believe this might happen.

When I got home, Bruce asked how it went. I looked at him, stunned. "We did it. I think the surgeon might actually call."

A flicker of hope started to emerge from a place I didn't recognize. Everything about this felt new. It had been so long since I had experienced raw hope, truly realizing everything important was out of my control.

Somewhere back in time I had started to believe the journey of my life was actually up to me. That I had a say in all the big things. That I could make my future whatever I wanted it to be. Now it was constantly being revealed to me that this mindset was a lie. I was realizing that the only thing I *really* have a say in is how I respond to the things that happen in my life. This realization was a huge step in the right direction, and one that laid the foundation for not only surviving but growing through it.

My cell phone rang.

I grabbed it and ran to the bedroom, slamming the door behind me, completely frazzled. My hands were shaking as I answered. It was *him*!

To be completely transparent, I expected to hear a brilliant accent or big scary words that I would have to pretend to know, but the first thing he said was, "I've taken a look at your scans, and I understand you've been told your tumor is inoperable." I nodded my head, but remembering he couldn't see me I said, "Yes, they want to drill a hole in my head to take a biopsy and treat the rest with radiation and chemo . . . "

He responded confidently, "Your tumor is absolutely operable, and I can get it all." My words escaped me, and my eyes welled up as I heard my husband occupying our kids in the next room.

"Are you serious?" is what eventually came out of my mouth. Of course he was serious. He is a freaking neurosurgeon.

He continued to walk me through the process and answer all of my questions before he respectfully asked if I would like to move forward. I lost my voice again in excitement before a laugh leaped from my heart, and I finally replied, "Yes!"

~~~

With a new plan and a new sense of hope, we arrived at the most beautiful beach house. This vacation had become our top priority, with all that loomed over our future. Our kids, our parents, and my brother would all escape reality for a week and recharge in our favorite beach town.

Summer vacation in Huntington Beach, California, is a tradition Bruce and I started in 2006 after we spent all our money on a big wedding and had to trade our dream Hawaiian honeymoon for a Best Western in the small California beach town. We ended up falling in love with the area. The residents have such a mellow, friendly vibe, and the city's rich surfing culture gives it a personality of its own. Since then, we've made it a priority to return every summer.

Our kids also started their own tradition of dragging us to the beach as soon as we dropped our bags in our rooms.

This year, it didn't feel like a chore to take them to see the ocean whilst trying to keep them from getting too cold, wet, or both. They never want to change into their swimsuits because they never plan on actually getting wet. But one thing always leads to another, and they end up walking back with sand in their underwear and chattering teeth.

But this time was different. I wasn't stressed out over preventing the inevitable. I was actually *in* the moment for the first time in a long time. As I watched, I realized something important. It wasn't just my moment; it was *their* moment too. They were living their own version of this story, and I wanted them to feel everything that was good about it.

With that tiny ounce of perspective, I watched and laughed with them as they put their toes into the wet sand, then started running across the water as it slid back into the ocean. The next thing I knew, they were jumping over tiny waves that broke closer and closer as the tide started coming in with the sunset.

By now Bruce and I were leaning into each other, his arms wrapped around my shoulders, keeping me warm while both our sons soaked themselves head to toe with pure magic in their eyes. I was freezing for them, but they were in glorious abandon of everything that wasn't bliss. The heavy burden on my heart was taken away with the wind coming off the water. I was glad I didn't intervene in their moment. It made mine that much sweeter.

~~~

The next morning Bruce and I rode our beach cruisers to a little white church on the corner a few blocks inland. We were greeted at the door, and as we found our seats in the beautiful traditional wooden pews, the service started with familiar contemporary worship songs. The drummer was jamming out, and so was the old lady in front of us. I love this part of visiting new churches because everyone is standing and I can get a good look at who showed up to be at the very same church I stumbled into, either by chance or divine will.

Everyone in this small sanctuary was wildly different—from fancy hats to torn T-shirts—but we were all here in the same place, about to hear the same message.

When the pastor spoke, he may as well have punched me in the gut. The message was about how God uses our adversities to put us on the fast track (or back on track) to live out His good and perfect intentions for us. I sat in that wooden pew with a pounding heart and tears pouring.

What good and perfect *anything* could come after this? Was there even an "after this?" I started to feel like maybe God's "good and perfect plan" wasn't for me but for Bruce, because my life was looking pretty short from where I was sitting. *But maybe, just maybe, I'll be the one to beat the odds. Maybe God will show off a little through my journey. Maybe I'll get to help Him do His "good and perfect" thing.*

When it was over I pulled myself together, and we both smiled at the pastor as we shook his hand on our way out. As we pedaled back to the beach house, our conversation bounced excitedly back and forth, recalling all the crazy parallels from his message to our lives. Sort of laughing, sort of stunned, we tried to wrap our heads around why we were meant to endure this.

Okay, God, you've got my attention.

~~~

Whenever we go out of town, Bruce always wakes up early and walks to the nearest coffee shop for his first-thing caffeine. I decided to tag along on the few occasions that our big fluffy, crisp white bed didn't trap me into another few hours of sleep.

On this particular morning we were careful not to wake the kids, sprawled peacefully across their air mattresses, as we tiptoed by them with sweatshirts in hand.

The tiny coffee shop, Primos, was just a short walk through the alley, and it sat, so originally nostalgic, next to all the new construction that had taken place over the years as our favorite small beach town became more popular to tourists.

I ordered an acai bowl, and Bruce got his usual black coffee. We opted for a picnic table on the patio and sat together facing the ocean. The surfers were already at it, catching wave after wave. They looked so free out there in the big ocean.

About halfway through my bowl I said to Bruce, "I'm going to do that."

He nodded his head in agreement. I pulled out my phone to find a surf school. He perked up. "You mean today?!"

"Yeah, wanna come?"

He knew I had already made my mind up, per usual, so he agreed, but it looked like it might rain so he said he'd wrangle the kids and cheer me on from the beach.

Surfing had always been a bucket-list item of mine, but I'd never taken lessons because we'd always get too "busy" with other activities, and every year I'd say, "Next year." How backwards is that? Too busy on vacation? Well, this year was different, and I was going to surf.

But I didn't want to surf just because I had a wild hair that day. I really wanted to surf because my dad had done it when I still looked up to him, before he went MIA and before he ever took the opportunity to teach me.

This was my way of making amends with him before it was too late—whether I was to die on the operating table or even if I lived a long life and he died first. I realize how morbid that sounds, but the last time I spoke to him I drew a line in the figurative sand. I stayed on my side. I couldn't accept his excuses anymore. I wanted a real conversation with him, I wanted to meet with him face to face, as adults, to try and understand each other. But his response when I asked to meet him six years ago was, "I don't know when I'll be in town again." He was so rock and roll, and not in a good way.

When I was growing up, my dad lived in Southern California and my mom lived in Arizona. Every summer I would get on a plane with nothing but my bright-pink duffle bag and a big Southwest Airlines button securing a pack of carbon-copy papers that flight attendants would sign off when I arrived at various checkpoints.

I spent my childhood summers in California with my dad and his new family. On occasion he'd take me to the beach to climb rocks and look for shells in his short jean cutoffs. He'd even swim and surf in those dang cutoffs. A real-life surfer, drummer, hang glider, and sprint car racer, all-in-one, could-have-been-awesome dad.

He'd take me on his adventures while I was visiting, and he was almost my hero, but instead he was selfish and manipulative, and although he never touched me, I saw how physical he got with my stepmom.

While growing up in two different states was painful in so many ways, looking back, I think life worked out just as it should have. For one, I learned exactly what I didn't want in a husband and the father of my kids.

I found a man with all the good qualities I loved about my dad, like his daredevil spirit and aptitude to work with his hands, but Bruce has not one inkling of the qualities I despise in my dad.

Bruce is genuine in every sense of the word. His intentions are good, and he owns his actions no matter what. Most of all, I love that he would fight like hell and sacrifice everything for his family. A far cry from "I don't know when I'll be in town again."

I'd had this realization for a while—that my dad had taught me what I didn't want—and I was grateful for that one real gift.

But he also gave me AFib. When I first realized it was a hereditary condition from my dad, I was pissed. It was like salt in a wound that I'd thought had healed.

Now that I was here in this moment, with a nick-of-time opportunity to beat cancer, I realized my broken heart was actually another "gift" from him in God's bigger plan.

Because without AFib, I would have never had the heart ablation. Without the heart ablation I would have never been given a precautionary CT scan for a post-op migraine. Without the CT scan, I would have never known I had cancer taking over my brain.

He gave me the gift of life, again, through bad genetics that ended up being the catalyst for catching my cancer before it was too late.

As I finished up the last bits of granola at the bottom of my bowl, I looked up at the surfers, forgave my dad for the thousandth time, gave my pain back to God for the thousandth time, and walked back to the beach house hand in hand with the love of my life. As gratitude entered my heart, there was even less room for the heaviness of worry. My spirit was getting lighter and lighter.

~~~

Our whole family came out to the surf school, and Brad, my stepdad, joined me. With everyone cheering from the beach, a happy-go-lucky teenage kid with long blond hair told me to get belly down on my board. It was time to see if I could actually stand on the thing.

A tiny wave came rolling in. The blondie gave my board a push at just the right time and yelled, "Now!" So I blindly jumped up, just like he'd shown me, and opened my eyes, and *I was surfing*!

When the wave gave up I surrendered into the water and closed my eyes as the incoming waves swallowed me and rushed through my hair. This moment of joy was interrupted by the thought that I might not have hair next summer, that I might not get to feel this again for a very long time, or ever.

An hour felt like five minutes, and our lesson was already over. I felt so alive and so grateful for the gifts this young kid had shared with me. I thought surely I had a gift to share too. Would I get to figure out what it was? Had I already shared it? They were the same thoughts that had haunted me from the little white church, but I decided to trust that there was a divine reason behind everyone's journey and that I would leave the world when it was right.

To let go and live in the moment is a choice. It's not a magical transformation. I had just started trying to become more aware of where my thoughts would go. If my thoughts wandered too far, I'd let them go and keep bringing myself back to the present moment—leaving the past behind me and leaving the future to God.

Later that afternoon, I was watching Bruce and the boys dig a giant hole for catching sand crabs when my phone rang. It was Rima.

I walked away from the ocean for better reception, and with my feet in piping-hot sand, we scheduled my pre-surgery brain-mapping scans so Dr. Sanai could remove the cancer without sacrificing my quality of life.

I walked back to share the news with my sunbathing family. My mom clapped and cheered. She was ecstatic, and I was in disbelief.

So I'm really going to let this guy pop off my skull and cut this thing out?

I looked at my kids, still digging in the big hole. I didn't even have to force it. A big smile came over me, and inside I knew, this was my shot.

7. HAPPIEST PLACE ON EARTH

Our truths are found in our perspectives.

Disneyland had been planned in advance, much to the dismay of Bruce, who wasn't excited about spending the day wrangling kids on sugar highs, standing in long lines, or all the other horror stories he'd heard about "The Happiest Place on Earth."

My fond memories of this place had been created as a child, so I was super excited to share the Disney magic with my kids—but I have to admit, I was a little nervous that I'd grown up too much to experience Disneyland like I had before. But even if the magic was gone for me, I knew this day was going to be filed away in their little memories, and I was going to make sure it was a good one.

I think it was this mentality that made all the difference. We were all so focused on hyping the kids and swapping stories of childhood memories that even Bruce started to come around to the idea that it might actually be fun.

When we arrived we had no idea we were all supposed to wear matching Disney swag. Apparently that's a thing, and none of us were hip to it. Swarms of bona fide Disney devotees walked in from the massive parking lot wearing Mickey ears, shirts, tutus—the works!

The kids were so excited as we made our way to this magical, mythical place, and when we stepped through the gate it was sensory overload. We didn't have a plan or a clue how to navigate the land of Disney, but my brother is apparently an undercover Disney nerd, because he knew where to go and when for optimal efficiency. He always surprises us with unusual skill sets that seem to come out of nowhere. I'd put money on him being a CIA agent living a double life.

All the lines felt short, and the rides felt invigorating. My little Grant was almost four and *way* too tall for his age—tall enough to ride Space Mountain. As soon as the ride began I knew it was a mistake. My brain was screaming, "Abort, abort! Get Grant to solid ground! Oh my gosh, he's going to fall out!" But my actual voice was screaming to Papa (AKA Brad) in the car behind me, "Hold on to him!"

Foreign noises were coming from my mouth out of straight-up fear, but I had to *pretend* it was laughter so Grant wouldn't be traumatized any more than he had to be. Do you know how hard that is? People must have thought I was a total nut job. I have to say, the photo at the end was priceless. I totally bought it.

As soon as we stepped off the ride, Grant asked if there were any rides for little kids. His eyes were still giant from his premature roller-coaster experience. How could I say no? We headed over to A Bug's Land in California Adventure, and playing with him in *his* element was just as fun. He was still our little guy, despite all the times I expected more. Watching his imagination run wild on the rides and get excited over the characters from *Cars* reminded me to embrace his littleness. I know every parent says it and it doesn't feel like it when you're in it—but it goes by so fast.

We tore up Disneyland. All of us.

We had fun in every corner of the park that day. It was one of the greatest days of my life, imprinted with actual magic and moments not easily forgotten. It was a gift that I am so grateful to have experienced.

As we pulled out of the parking lot, the backseat was unusually quiet. I looked back, expecting to see sleeping kids. Grant was out like a light, but Tavin was crying.

"What's wrong?" I asked him, a little worried.

"I don't know why I'm crying. I'm just so—happy." Right then life paused.

Coming from Tavin, this was exceptional. Tavin is my difficult child, not because he's ill-willed, but because he's *strong*-willed. He is going to do incredible things in his life. The sky's the limit for that kid, but parenting that kind of kid—that is complicated. We—him included—try so hard to direct his intense energy into positivity versus the easy route of negativity. For him to surrender to an overjoyed state was a breakthrough for both of us.

With that, I felt a deep sense of relief in my heart. *We're going to be okay at the end of the day—at the end of life.*

8. PREPARING TO DIE

Be a willow, not an oak.

Home and settled from our epic trip, I finally received a call back from the first hospital—the one I had been trying to schedule a biopsy with since before vacation and the same group that deemed my brain tumor "inoperable." *Now* they wanted to schedule my biopsy.

I politely refused and told them I was going to move forward with a second opinion. I don't think they get that kind of response often, because the lady on the other end of the line didn't quite know what to say. I was kind of expecting a human-to-human celebratory exchange of excitement when I told her I found someone who could operate on the "inoperable" tumor, but instead she couldn't get off the phone and on to her next to-do fast enough. My decision was secured in that moment.

~~~

In the small waiting room at the Barrow Outpatient Imaging Center, I was freaking out inside.

What if they find that my tumor has grown since the last scan before vacation and the doctor can't operate anymore? Can I really get in that tiny tube with the face cage again?

49

I was almost too enthralled in my own pity party to notice a woman sitting alone just a few seats to my right. I finally noticed her when a technician in scrubs came out holding a little boy about Grant's age and handed him to her. He was her son. My heart sank for both of them, and I realized in that exact moment that I was not in the worst seat in that waiting room. I would sit in this seat a thousand times to protect my kids from it.

I thanked God in that moment that *I* was the one who was meant for this. It was perfect that it was me. I was grateful for this truth. I'd get in that tiny tube with the face cage, I'd put myself on that operating table, and I'd be the one who faced mortality. It was meant for *me*, and I'd do it *all*.

When the technician called me back, I was more ready for that scan than anything else in my life. I walked with purpose toward the security doors, through to the big room with the big MRI machine staring back at me, already making the high-pitched droplet noises I wasn't yet accustomed to.

I proceeded to lay down on the sliding table, and to my surprise, the technician handed me a pair of goggles that played video. "Today's MRI is going to be pretty fun, actually," she said to me. "I saw on your chart that you're claustrophobic, but you won't even realize you're in the machine with these on." I was skeptical.

She secured those crazy goggles and laid me down as usual, with my legs propped up. They always ask if you want a blanket, because the machine is freezing, with a constant flow of cold air inside, but I always decline. There was barely room for me in that thing, let alone a blanket.

She held onto my arm as she slid me all the way back into the machine. My heart started pounding so hard that my body was physically moving with each giant heartbeat. I could even *hear* my heartbeat, but the sound of fear was interrupted by the technician in the tiny tube speakers: "Can you hear me, honey?" I wasn't sure if she could hear *me*, but I replied "Yes" anyway.

"What do you want to watch in your goggles while I do the first part? Do you like funny videos or animals or something?"

My immediate reply was, "Animal videos, please." I felt like such a child, but hey, she asked! As the MRI machine ran the first scans I watched glorious YouTube videos of cats and dogs being adorable and hilarious.

Next, she showed me some images and asked me questions about them and also asked me to move various parts of my body during the second part of the scan. Dr. Sanai would use all of this information to get as much of the surrounding tissue as possible, to increase the odds of getting every last ugly cancer cell when he operated.

The brain-mapping session was a success—and the best experience I've had in that tiny tube to date.

The technician pulled me out of the MRI machine quickly, knowing my level of claustrophobia, and praised my willpower to stay put. Once the face cage was off she helped me sit up. I think she could tell my heart was heavy, because she took a moment to talk with me. I asked her how the mapping had gone and how it worked. I told her I was afraid, because of where the tumor was, that the procedure might change how I see the world and how I fit in it. She couldn't tell me any news about what she saw, but she helped me understand that the surgery would not change who I was. The cancer had already done its damage, and the surgery would simply prevent it from doing more... even if it did mean removing part of my brain.

This was the part that freaked me out the most about the surgery. The cancer wasn't an external tumor that was to be cut off; it had infiltrated my actual brain. The chunk of bad brain cells had to be removed in order to protect the rest of my brain.

As I contemplated this, she took me by surprise with her final thoughts on my situation.

"You're like a willow tree."

I didn't get it, but I nodded my head as if I did.

"I know you're a willow, because I can tell that you're strong. You wouldn't know it by looking at you, but you wouldn't know it by looking at a willow either—with their thin, flowy branches. But it's good that you're a willow and not a big strong oak tree. Oak trees look the part, but which tree do you think can withstand the harshest storm? The willow. Because its branches don't break; they bend, just like you."

That was exactly what I needed to hear, and our conversation was on my mind constantly leading up to the surgery. Whenever I felt overwhelmed, I chose the willow. Bending is the alternative to breaking.

The night before the big surgery, I tried to avoid the thoughts of what was actually going to happen in the operating room. Instead, I focused on what I wanted my family to know—just in case.

Every few months or so since they were born, I have written to my sons about their lives, to give them a glimpse of their childhood narrative, life perspectives through our journey, and of course a little advice sprinkled in here and there. These were the journals I'd told Cidney about, the ones that I had wondered might be a sign of a pre-destined ending. If I wasn't going to make it out of surgery alive or if I woke up with brain damage that changed me, this would be my final entry... as me.

    8/5/15 This entry will be in both of
    your journals.

    It's safe to say a million things
    have happened since I last wrote.
    Tavin, today you pulled me into my
    room for a "just us" talk. It was

about some scary games you didn't want Grant to see in the Apple App Store. You are so adorable to me. Grant, you were extra grumpy when you woke up from your nap today but came to when we all got ready for your fave, Peter Piper Pizza. It made my heart melt to watch you sucking your two middle fingers, watching the big kids play the giant games. You want to be big, but you're still my baby. I had a good day with you both, but now I have to tell you about something hard.

Before our beach trip this year, I was diagnosed with a brain tumor. It was an act of God that they even found it. I'd had a cardiac ablation a week earlier due to a random bout of AFib. I was having trouble seeing due to a migraine (the only one I've ever experienced), and Dad was on shift, so Aki took me to the hospital because headache and vision problems could be a sign of stroke. I was sure it was just a migraine and made her take me home, but when we got home it got worse and I started having more vision problems, so I gave in and let her take me. Scans revealed that I didn't have a stroke . . . they're saying it's cancer.

I delayed surgery so we could still go to the beach and Disneyland like we had planned and maybe even get back to normal for a bit. This time has made me realize how precious and unpredictable life is.

Right now you are young, but I wanted to preserve these words in your journals . . . because they are so important.

I won't always be with you physically. I wish I could live with you forever and ever on this earth and love on you throughout all the seasons of your life. But God takes each of us at His perfect time. I hope mine isn't for many, many more years, but I want you to know that when He takes me, my love will live on. The Bible says, "and now these three remain: faith, hope, and love. But the greatest of these is love." Love is what binds us, and I know you will feel my love in your soul while we are apart.

Whenever you walk on the shoreline, think of me. I loved introducing you both to the ocean and seeing your reaction to just how big and powerful it was. I used to hold your tiny hands and jump over the wake that

```
washed in just over our feet. Tavin,
by now you have become more adven-
turous than I'm comfortable with in
the ocean, and it takes my breath
away, but I'm in awe of your bravery.
Grant, you still hold on SO TIGHT to
my fingers, and I cherish it because
I know you'll be out there soon. I
didn't think I could love so
much . . . you will always have my
love . . . forever and ever.

XOXO
Mom
```

~~~

It was still dark outside when we left for the hospital the next morning. I prayed in the car, once again, for Dr. Sanai and everyone who would be in my operating room that morning.

When we got there, my nurse let me know that everyone who was scheduled for my surgery was present and getting ready. She asked if I had any questions for the surgeon.

"Can I see him?"

After all, we hadn't properly met, and he was about to cut into my brain. Dr. Sanai arrived at my bed with a look on his face like maybe he thought I was backing out, but I just wanted to meet him. I think he was relieved by my intentions, but I also got the vibe that maybe I had taken him out of the zone, so I kept it short and let him get back to his prep.

All suited up in my backless gown and hospital socks, I saw Clendon and Ila, family friends whom I hadn't seen in ages, just across the aisle. Clendon was also a firefighter, so he and Bruce happened to know each other as well. Both our families caught up a bit and brought a little life and laughter to that dreary pre-op room with anxious patients all lined up and ready to get their heads cut open.

He calmed my nerves with his larger-than-life confidence. "If I can do this as many times as I have, you can do it too." I can't remember what number surgery this was for him, but he was a pro by now, so I chose to believe him.

His wife, Ila, stayed with my mom and Bruce as they rolled me back.

I was pushed down a white hall, through double doors that led to a secure area, where we turned into a sterile room with a big table, lights, a tray of instruments, and the OR staff ready in their gowns, hats, and gloves.

I said hello, because I had no idea what to say to people who were about to play with my brain! We were about to get *real* intimate, and I wanted them to see me as a *real* person. I think I tried to tell them everything I could about my life and what I had to live for as I scooted from my roller bed onto the OR table, trying not to flash everyone.

I was so wrapped up in making a claim for my life that I started to put my head where my feet were supposed to go. The sweet OR nurse corrected me and helped me get situated.

To my right side was the pretty anesthesiologist (whom I had already spoken with in pre-op about my kids and all I had to live for). She was holding a mask and asked if I was ready. I replied with a question: "Is that really going to knock me out?" She promised it would and asked me to count back from ten.

"Okay, let's do this. Ten, nine, eight, seven . . . "

9. CHOSEN TO LIVE

Life is a purposeful and extravagant gift.

I opened my eyes with quick euphoric blinks as I frantically looked for something, *anything* to focus on. I heard a nurse behind the curtain to my left hollering loudly to rouse her patient. I couldn't find my voice yet but lay there in my heavy body, silently shouting, *I'm alive!*

God still wanted me here. Everything leading up to this moment had been on purpose. I could see, looking backwards, how it all fit together. My faith was confirmed in that moment. Moving forward, I would need to choose to believe that *all* the parts of my life would come together in imperfectly perfect order, just like this, even if I couldn't see the ending. *Faith. I get it now. Choosing to believe in what I can't see* yet.

I was completely ecstatic for the privilege to live. For the privilege to remain in this life with my family and to finish out my purpose, whatever that would turn out to be. I did know that, whatever it was, I would do my part. I believe wholeheartedly that every opportunity we are given is a chance to do something significant, but only if we do our part. Each of us is gifted with a potential that exceeds what we can imagine. It is our duty to ourselves, and to our maker, to develop it.

Of course, circumstances can prompt us, but it's the extra work, the hard parts where others give up, that's the difference maker in seizing an opportunity or missing it. This was one hell of an opportunity. I was taking it like my life depended on it. And when it came to all the hard parts that were to come—bring it. It's safe to say I woke up with a fire in my belly.

Overwhelmed at the realization of my mere existence, I decided to see what I was working with. The first thing I did was focus my eyes on a poster that was hanging directly in front of my bed. *Can I make sense of it?* I started small. Letters. I fixed my eyes on whichever letter my gaze led me to; I said its name to myself. Then another and another. *I know letters!*

Words. I could read words too! Sentences. I read a freaking sentence to myself! My internal dialogue was filled with answers and solutions to every test I put myself through, and I was cheering myself on as I went. A far cry from that usual internal dialogue of "Not good enough." Today my internal voice thought I was beyond amazing.

Okay, Andy, pull it together. It's time to get serious. I re-focused my attention on the nurse behind the curtain next to me, still shouting at her patient, asking him or her to make a fist and move his feet. I followed all of her instructions successfully, realizing I could move *all* of my body. In pure joy, I raised my gaze toward the ceiling, eyes welling, with a silent thank-you.

But wait! Could I talk *out loud*? I looked ahead, focused on the vital task, and mustered a raspy, "Hello."

I'm not sure if my nurse heard me or if it was a coincidence, but as she came around the other side of the curtain, she gave me a hello back with a smile.

I wanted to jump out of bed and hug her. My body was still too heavy, or I might have tried.

As I was celebrating life, my glorious, magnificent, esteemed neurosurgeon was off to tell my family the good news.

I didn't know it, but Caitlin, another one of my dear friends from high school; our fire family; gym friends; and both Julia and her husband had spent a considerable amount of time waiting, praying, and comforting my mom and Bruce. Uncle Larry had even stopped by with bagels for everyone. Our support system was formed organically in the waiting room that morning, and it would grow so much from there.

Dr. Sanai pulled Bruce and my mom into a small room just off the waiting room. He broke the silence with, "Surgery went as expected, with no surprises."

There would be a post-op scan to look for any remaining signs of cancer, but he was confident. An immediate weight was lifted, and as my mom celebrated, Bruce was getting anxious to see me. He shared with me later how that moment was one of his happiest but also his scariest. He didn't know what to expect and was afraid I might have limitations or memory loss or be a different person altogether.

I couldn't wait to see Bruce either. To show him I was still here, I was pretty amazing—and I was really high. I was actually extremely high. I don't know if I was high on the drugs they gave me or if I was high on life—maybe both—but I was definitely high. So I decided to prank him.

When he and my mom walked through the curtain, looking at me like a fragile china doll, I yelled, "What the hell!"

I saw him reliving the last time I met him with those words, after my little ol' heart ablation, and his face immediately went pale with worry—like maybe his fears about my mental stability were coming true. I couldn't keep a straight face and busted up laughing. Relief washed over him like a tidal wave. If I hadn't been lying there in that hospital bed, looking so pathetic, I think he would have given it right back to me, but I took advantage of the moment because I could. I wanted him to know my brain still worked, I remembered things, and I was hilarious, maybe more now than ever. I was *so* happy!

After the jokes were out of the way, he and my mom went straight to examining the long incision that started at the top of my head and followed the shape of a *C* to its end behind my right ear. My mom pointed out the braids that one of the OR nurses must have put in my longer-than-usual hair, keeping my wound accessible. I quite honestly had thought I'd wake up with a shaved head, or at least half a shaved head, so this was a real bonus to being alive with all my skills and my amazing sense of humor.

"I almost forgot! Look what I can do!"

I held up both my hands in a hook grip, used for weightlifting.

"Take a picture and send it to my coach. I'm going to start training for a meet when I get out of here."

My mom and Bruce looked at me like I was dreaming just a little too big, too fast—but I knew I wasn't. I was on a whole new level now.

Bruce took my picture as requested and showed it to me. I was truly surprised at how I looked. *That girl in the picture is not the same girl sitting here. She looks drained and tired. I am exuberant!*

Looking back now, it's funny how that works. In the very first, raw moments, my outside self had to catch up with my inside self. But it wouldn't be long before they would flip-flop. We'll get to that later.

"There's more people who want to see how you're doing," my mom mentioned as more of a question than a statement.

"Bring them in!" I wanted to let everyone know I was okay and thank them for being there for us.

Two by two, my tribe of family and friends were allowed back to post-op to offer a hug and positive affirmations.

When Caitlin came back I squeezed her hand hard. She's an OR nurse, so I wanted her to feel my strength. I wanted her to know I had passed the test. I wanted to reassure her that everything was going to be okay.

Caitlin and I go *way* back. She was the friend I could be extra silly with. We would dance like no one was watching, fall off our seats laughing, and wear China hats to the bowling alley, and as we got a little older, we'd share a bottle of Boone's Farm with two straws. We were (and still are) a little odd—and we love it.

But after all this time we'd spent apart—growing up and raising our families—time couldn't put distance between our hearts. Even if it meant spending the morning in rush-hour traffic after she'd been called in for a 3 a.m. surgery at a hospital across town. I was humbled by her presence. Once again I was reminded how special and important my existing relationships were, and as soon as I got out of this place, I was going to be more intentional in this way and many others.

"Okay, everyone, time to say your goodbyes." The OR nurse was on a mission to get me to ICU and had been patient long enough. "This girl needs to get some rest!"

ICU was a breeze. It felt like a VIP lounge, minus the privacy. I was tended to by the kindest, most empathetic people God ever put on this earth. I would catch myself apologizing for needing anything, but they would insist. Everyone was in awe of my high spirits. Yeah, probably still high on meds, but nonetheless.

I slept for a *long* time after getting settled in, and I felt strong afterward. Strong enough to try and walk. It was a slow walk, and Bruce needed to hold me steady, but I rocked that walk.

Recovery was remarkably quick, and I graduated to a regular room the very next day, with other noncritical brain patients. Finally, I was going to be able to see my kids.

Bruce brought them up with him first thing the next morning. When their little heads peeked around the door, I put my hands out to motion them over with a big smile. I swear they had grown since I'd last seen them a few days ago. Tavin, still not one for all things medical, let Grant run ahead. He grabbed my hand and looked at me with a shy smile. I put my other hand around his to secure it. The hand he was holding was still numb from brain swelling. I couldn't feel him at all. It was as though I was wearing heavy gloves. My first reality check. I looked down at his chubby little hand with dimples for knuckles and then back at his big eyes. I remembered what his hands felt like, but I wanted more than a memory. I gave his hand a kiss to hide my sadness, and I mustered a big smile on the way up.

Bruce nudged Tavin toward my bed. I pulled him in for a hug and a kiss.

"Did they fix your brain?"

His eyes were so big and curious.

"They did!"

Right then Dr. Sanai walked in the room. The man, the myth, the legend.

He gave me the same report Bruce had retold about their conversation, but hearing it straight from him, surrounded by my family—my kids— brought a flood of emotion. Bruce threw any rules of formality out the window and hugged the man who had changed our lives. Surprised but not thrown off his game, Dr. Sanai didn't forget to mention that I'd be sent for a final MRI to verify the results. He assured us that the weakness and numbness in my hand was from swelling and should feel normal soon enough. On his way out, he reached down and gave my left shin a firm squeeze with a smile. "You're going to be just fine."

I believed him wholeheartedly, not just because he was the smartest person I'd ever met, but because I believed he was heaven-sent. I believed our lives had intersected for a divine purpose.

Before my mom left with the kids, they took turns dropping a lacrosse ball in my hand. Tavin was giving me points for every time I could hold onto it and got increasingly excited as I reached new "high scores." I cherished every second.

Later on, I was still basking in a state of peaceful happiness when I was greeted by a new visitor, my friend Amanda. We'd first met at the gym, and our kids had become fast friends, as had we. We share a love for food, and she and her husband sure did make my culinary experience at the hospital a positive one with a huge bag of goodies from Whole Foods. Thank you, baby Jesus, for that food!

I could tell she was a little nervous to see me in this setting, so I did my best to show her how well I was doing. But just as she got there, my left thumb started to twitch. I held it up to show her, and we both were perplexed at how odd that was. The twitch quickly moved up my arm, and my arm began to shake uncontrollably. My muscles spasmed all the way up to my neck, but just on the left side. I was having a seizure. I heard Amanda call for Bruce, who was in the hallway on the phone, and he ran in, only to run back out to yell, "She's having a seizure!" My nurse rushed in, and Bruce put his hand on my seizing shoulder. I was conscious the whole time. I tried to talk but could only grunt. I managed to grunt something that sounded like "Hold me" to him, and he wrapped his arms around me and laid his body on top of mine.

His weight on me was the only comfort I found in that moment. I was like a marionette doll being shaken with tangled strings. I had no control over what was happening to me. The seizure was violent and intrusive. Brain surgery I could do.

Seizures, on the other hand, scared the hell out of me. I honestly thought I was dying, trapped inside a body that wouldn't comply—not even my voice.

Slowly my convulsions started to subside, and the jerks became less intense and eventually stopped, leaving me out of breath, sweating, and aching, with a giant headache. My nurse moved fast, calling for a scan, stat. Her little body turned into Wonder Woman mode as she flipped up the rails on my bed and ran me down the hallway.

I saw Amanda, with her back pressed against the wall, on my way out. I felt like a failure. I had been doing so well. I had just told her I was fine. Then I'd had a seizure on her. Was this the last time she'd see me? Would her last memory of me be *that*?

When I got to the MRI room, a small team was standing by, ready to lift me onto the sliding table and lock my head into the face cage. I felt like a crashed race car being addressed by a NASCAR pit crew. These people moved faster than I could understand what was happening to me.

Inside the MRI machine, the noise from the scan was excruciating. I kept my eyes closed to combat the pain *and* claustrophobia. When it was over, even the silence hurt. I was glad to be out.

On our way back to my room, my thumb started twitching again.

"I don't want to freak anyone out," I said to my nurse and one of the techs from the MRI room, who were walking my bed back down the hallway toward my room, "but I think I'm going to have another seizure."

I showed them my twitching thumb, and right then, that same familiar rush came over my body that signaled I was no longer in control. They were almost to my room, so they moved quickly, and as we turned the corner, it happened again. Just like before. Bruce was still in my room, waiting for me to return. He draped himself over me again, and inside all that external shaking, my spirit couldn't handle any more. It broke.

When the seizure was over, my tiny Wonder Woman nurse asked if she could pray over me. I allowed it, without the strength to say my own prayer.

The seizures turned out to be another side effect of brain swelling. Apparently I had ignored all the possible side effects that didn't have to do with me dying. I was not prepared for what experiencing a seizure would do to me mentally. I was filled with anxiety. When the seizures were over it would take a while for me to have control over my left arm again, and that scared me. After all the elation of having a fully functioning body, I feared it would be taken from me, right when I finally had gratitude for it.

I was given meds to suppress the seizures and was sent back to ICU.

Bruce eventually had to relieve his mom after a long day with the kids. My mom, being the matriarch she is, came to oversee my care in the night while he got some much-needed rest.

I thought I was ready for him to leave, but without my Bruce's steady energy, I started to panic.

"I'm going backwards! Am I ever going to get out of here?"

I finally realized what fighting for your life felt like. It wasn't a physical fight. It was a mental one. It seemed that my body would follow whatever my mental state would initiate. I could see how this was playing out. I could see that my anxiety and negativity was hurting my progress, but I couldn't rein it in. I couldn't stop crying.

My mom saw me spiraling and called the only person she knew who'd had a brain tumor removed and lived to thrive: John, my former PR colleague's husband.

John is an example of someone who hasn't let his circumstances slow him down ever. He's done a friggin' Iron Man race, for heaven's sake! But there was a time when he couldn't even walk. He, too, had a brain tumor removed at Barrow. When he heard the tone in my mom's voice, he drove straight over. Never mind that it was way past visiting hours. This was happening.

To put this selfless act into perspective, I hadn't seen John in maybe *years*. But there are just some people who feel like family, and he and his wife, Charlotte, are those kind of people.

He walked in the room and smiled. My nerves were running rampant as I probed him for details about what he'd gone through and how he did it.

He said, "You'll take a few steps forward and a few steps back, but you'll slowly keep moving ahead."

For John, it took him a year and a half to get to function at 90 percent. Knowing how far he's come, it may have taken some persistence on the front end, but look at the guy now. He's a lean, mean Iron Man racing machine.

His story gave me hope.

I was quiet—soaking in what he had said. We all were quiet. This moment of stillness brought a sense of peace back into my heart.

He didn't have to come that night. He didn't have to walk back into the Barrow ICU and relive all the memories of that painful time. But he did. And he made a significant contribution to my recovery that night, in a small, dark, glass room.

The next morning brought news that I would get to go back to the recovery unit . . . a step forward.

Bruce arrived in time for the transition, and once we were settled our friends Scott and Stephanie came to visit. Scott is another friend who endured a brain tumor. What are the chances? Scott also had experience with seizures—one I had already known about because it occurred at the gym where I coach, but he also told stories about other very inopportune seizure experiences with pure hilarity. It was just part of his life now. He didn't feel sorry for himself at all. He wasn't scared of the next one. He was unshakable, pun totally intended. If I continued to have seizures I hoped I could find the strength to handle them the way he did.

When they left, I felt a little less fragile. Bruce suggested I go for a walk. I think he wanted to remind me of what I *could* do. I was scared, though. What if I slipped and fell on my head and it cracked wide open? What if, after all that had happened, *that* was how I went out?

In my reluctance, I chose to walk any-way... another step forward.

I reminded myself once again, *I'm here on purpose. I've made it this far, and I still have a lot of work to do if I want to get back to where I was before.* Where I was before... my temporary jolt of confidence was about to take a turn.

It's an interesting concept to try to get back to the person I was *before*, because right up until I put myself on that operating table I still never felt "good enough." Before all of this, I hadn't been sure I was a good enough mom to equip my kids with a Rolodex of important lessons and memories to help them through life. I hadn't been sure I was a good enough business owner to take my company to the next level. I hadn't even been sure I'd ever be strong or talented enough in the gym to reach my goals or help others reach theirs.

My growth had been stunted for far too long in self-doubt. I didn't realize what I already had or how far along I had already come. I had put so much pressure on myself to reach such broad, grandiose goals that I had lost what could have been my truest potential. I needed to dial in my mindset and decide what I *really* wanted out of my life now that I had a second chance.

Settled back in my room, I grabbed my phone to see for myself if there was any truth to the "not good enough" mentality that I'd been owning for so long. Opening my photos, I was fully expecting that little jerk voice in my head to narrate negative critiques of my life right up to this point in time. But the little voice that showed up was just as surprised as I was at what was on the screen.

I saw our recent vacation and the looks on my kids' faces. I saw screenshots of ideas I wanted to explore in my business, and I saw a video of me doing a crazy complex of six pull-ups, four chest-to-bar pull-ups, and two muscle-ups—unbroken. I had originally recorded that video as a critique. I was upset at my performance that day. Not because I couldn't do it, but because I was having timing issues and had "chicken winged" my muscle-ups.

This was what I spent my energy being upset about?

Seriously, old Andy, cry me a river.

I was amazed at myself. Why again was all of this not good enough?

These images gave me confidence to know what was possible, and my situation gave me perspective to know what I was lacking before. I was determined to rise up from this even better.

So I pushed myself to walk more. I even started getting to know my neighbors. Well, I got to know the looks of them.

The guy a few doors down to the right was in a contraption that looked like a cage. Or maybe an adult playpen. He wasn't going to be walking with me. I wasn't sure he'd ever get the chance. But here I was walking by his door—showing off.

Just like that, a new feeling started settling in: guilt.

I felt guilty that I could do things and that I could think straight. That I had gotten cancer but I got to keep my hair.

I experienced so many highs and lows in this short period of time after surgery, but so did my loved ones. Chris, my other brother from my dad, had come to visit me a couple times. We had a newer relationship, so we were still getting to know each other. When we had first "met" for the first time since childhood, I was pregnant with Grant and he was getting ready to join the army. We mostly communicated through letters in the early part of our relationship. He knew my past with our dad was complicated, and he was wrestling with what his part in that situation was now. If I was on my deathbed, was it his responsibility to reunite us? What was the right thing to do here? In the end, he gave that responsibility back over to me as I got stronger and it was clear I had made it out of the woods. Personally, I had already thought about it but couldn't think of any reasons that outweighed what was in my heart, so I left well enough alone. I had enough on my plate.

In the moments of fear or sadness, Bruce would read the Bible to me. One day he read a verse that slapped me in the face.

> But those who hope in the Lord will renew their strength. They will soar on wings like eagles; they will run and not grow weary, they will walk and not be faint.
>
> Isaiah 40:31

> Do not fear, for I am with you. Do not be dismayed, for I am your God. I will strengthen you and help you. I will uphold you with my righteous right hand.
>
> Isaiah 41:10

I thanked God for reminding me that I was not alone. When my strength ran out I could look to my maker—the maker of everything.

You want to help me. You brought me here to live. If You hadn't, all of this perspective would be for nothing. I know You want me to use it—I will.

When I finished processing these verses, I asked Bruce to write them down for me. That small piece of paper stayed on my tray for the remainder of my stay at the hospital, and it followed me home. I still have it and pull it out when I'm feeling lost.

It was mid-August when I got to come home. Well, to our in-between rental home. We had just dug ourselves out of a financial mess by living in the backyard at my in-laws'—in a trailer, nonetheless. We had even celebrated the boys' first and fourth birthdays there. It was not an ideal situation, but it allowed us to pay off all our debt and sock away money for our future forever home. At exactly one year and one day, we had made the transition into a rental home.

After looking at rentals that smelled funny, had bright-colored walls, or were falling apart, Bruce showed me the house I would be coming home to that day. At first glance I hated it, but when I walked inside, a giant window showed off a waterfront view. This house shared a small neighborhood lake with about twenty other homes. Water! He knew that would be the kicker. That little lake rental became our new home.

The first thing I did when we got home that afternoon was walk through the backyard gate, straight to the patio, and sit in my late uncle Joe's rocking chair. It was the same rocking chair he had rocked me in as a baby before he passed on. The ducks were being obnoxiously loud as usual, but today it was music to my ears. I was tired of being inside. I didn't even care that it was one hundred plus degrees outside in Arizona. I soaked it all in and dozed off for the most refreshing nap I'd taken in my life. I had made it.

10. THE COMEBACK

Accepting help is accepting love.

I missed my kids' first day of school. Grant was starting preschool, and Tavin was starting first grade. I still couldn't tie my pajama pants, cut food, or type. My brain was *still* swollen, and that meant I still had some limitations to deal with. I had to ask for help, a lot. It was humbling to have my food cut for me, my shoes tied for me, and other odds and ends that required two hands. I'm a doer, and when you tell the doer they can't do something, they try to do it anyway. This was extremely frustrating but was ultimately what helped me heal my body so quickly. I kept trying to do all the things over and over again . . . until it got too dangerous or too time-consuming.

Bruce is also a doer. You can imagine a marriage when both people are trying to "do." We sometimes (okay, most of the time) get in each other's way by doing too much or doing for the other when the other is trying to do too. It's ridiculous, really. But if he weren't a doer, I would have had a really hard time accepting his help. After failing over and over at something, I'd eventually let him help me, because I knew he wanted to.

When friends and family wanted to help us, we naturally resisted. But the reality was, we did need help. My mom knew it too and set up a food tidings calendar so we wouldn't have to worry about meals as we adjusted and recovered. To be honest, this kind of freaked us out. People have their own lives to tend to, and our burden wasn't theirs to carry. But people were asking for ways to help. They wanted to help. Bringing us dinner was how they could show up for us. I realized that not letting our friends help and closing off our burden to the people we cared about was equivalent to shutting them out. We would be frustrating other doers.

Once the meals started coming in, we got more comfortable with the daily visitors and eventually started to enjoy the company and the variety of food. Most of the visitors were from the gym, and it was an added bonus getting to know them better. Man, I know some really great people.

In the process of learning how to accept help, I got a message from my friends Stephanie and Laura asking if they could come over and clean my house.

What?! No way. I clean my own house. I have two little boys. They're gross. No way! I don't think we're at that level of closeness to let them see my nooks and crannies.

But then I thought about it from their perspective. Stephanie is the most sentimental and empathetic person you will ever meet. She cares so deeply for others. Laura is a firefighter on the same department as Bruce, and it is ingrained into who she is a person to help others, especially her fire family.

I told Bruce what they wanted to do for us. He had the same initial reaction as I did. We were both stunned that people would ask to clean our house, but we came around to the idea and took the opportunity to leave our mess to these amazing people, while we went for a drive up north to cooler weather for the day. Like a date. Like there was some sense of normalcy in our life, even if just for a day. That precious memory wouldn't exist if we hadn't let them help us.

~~~

My first time back at the gym was a Saturday morning, when we have our biggest turnout of the week. I wanted to show up in person to thank everyone for the cards, well-wishes, prayers, and so much more. When the class started, Bruce joined them, and I found a rower to sit on. My goal was to just move for forty-five minutes. It could be slow, and I could stop, but I needed to stay strapped in. That was my goal. For forty-five minutes I moved at a snail's pace, but everyone looked at me like I was magic.

I did my own version of PT, which started out with jumping up to the bars and holding on for a second every day, working up to twenty-five, fifty, then one hundred. Sometimes I missed, but it helped my hand-eye coordination and grip strength immensely. Then I graduated to jumping up to the rings. This was harder because they move, but I mastered it. Then I tried kipping on the rings. Then one day I wanted to try a muscle-up. To be safe I put mats under the rings. Fully expecting to lose control and fall on my face, I told myself, "Do it anyway."

Moments later I was up on top of the rings. Then I did another to make sure I wasn't dreaming. I was beyond surprised. This gave me the confidence I needed to stop playing it safe and keep testing my limits.

I eventually was able to participate in a class. The workout called for front rack lunges, which means placing a weighted barbell on your shoulders from the front with elbows up to create a "rack." I soon realized that my legs didn't have the coordination or strength to lunge with much weight yet. My friend and coach wouldn't let me quit on the movement. He was actually a physical-therapy student and had a pocket full of ideas that would help me that day and many to come. He suggested I lunge backward—and I could! I was able to actually do the workout with the class and walk away in triumph instead of defeat. Just one more skill to work on.

Speaking of which, my fine-motor skills still needed a little fine-tuning. I'm a huge fan of friendship bracelets, mantra bracelets—all bracelets, really. I hardly take them off. They're like wearing a reminder of who you love or what you aspire to. I decided to make hundreds of friendship bracelets for gym friends, to not only give my hands some practice but to thank them for supporting me.

I was so humbled by the people in my life. I'm not special—I just know special people. What they do is love. Every time I see one of the many who brought us a meal, I feel love. Every time I clean my own toilets, I remember Stephanie and Laura, and I feel love. Every time I reach into my nightstand for a pen and see the big pile of notes and cards I saved, I feel love.

The humbling that each of these acts brought me taught me gratitude for others like I had never experienced before. I had backup. I had a friggin' army. I felt scrappier than ever—feisty, even. This was my moment to thrive in the face of adversity, as they say.

I wouldn't say I eased back into life as much as I jumped back in. Progress motivated me, and I was doing exceptionally well in the gym, so I poured all my focus in that direction. On one occasion I decided to try handstand pushups. That's when you do a handstand against a wall, then lower yourself into a headstand and then push back into a handstand. Upon a sudden, fierce headache, I was slapped back to reality. My skull wasn't exactly ready for that kind of pressure.

To make sure I hadn't done any real damage, I checked in with Jacki, Dr. Sanai's new nurse navigator. Rima had moved into a different position, but I latched onto Jacki just the same. She reminded me that the plate they had used to secure my skull back together was there to protect it from cracking open, so my head was fine—but while things were still healing, I should chill on the headstand stuff. I guess back when everyone had told me I was cleared for all activities, they hadn't considered that I'd be testing out their handiwork with handstand pushups.

Despite this little reality check, I was very optimistic about my recovery and about getting back to the old me in record time. Brain cancer would be just a blip in my long, productive life. The only thing that disrupted this fairy tale I was buying into was a little bit of survivor's guilt that crept in sometimes.

One occasion that this guilt showed up in full force was at a Pita Jungle where I'd met my friend Lynda for lunch. One of her best friends had recently overcome breast cancer. Lynda is an amazing photographer, and I remembered the beautiful, empowering photos that she had taken of her friend without a headscarf on. She had seen what real strength looked like through her lens, and here I sat with all my hair. I felt like a fraud. Like I had gotten a get-out-of-cancer-free card. I admitted to her that I thought I had it too easy. She of course disagreed, but I remember driving away from lunch that day knowing it wasn't right.

11. THE SETBACK

Rock bottom is where resilience is born.

I woke up excited for my first official day back to work. Then I looked in the mirror. The right side of my face was huge. A portion of my scar was swollen too. One area felt hard, and another felt sunken in and soft. I freaked out.

Is my head caving in?! Is my brain coming out?!

I immediately called Jacki. I think we were really starting to bond by this point, with me checking in—yet again. I promise I'm not a hypochondriac. But lately, every time I had convinced myself something was nothing, it had turned out to be something *huge*.

She calmed my nerves anyway and explained that swelling and settling could still happen at this point in my healing, but she said to let her know if anything progressed or changed.

I had done a bunch of GHD sit-ups the day before; maybe that had done it. Maybe I was taking things a little too far, too quickly in the gym. Who did I think I was, swinging my head around like that after I'd just had a piece of my brain removed? Everything was all weird in there. I even heard weird noises inside my head, as fluids were still equalizing. It was like my brain was whispering to me sometimes, reminding me of what I'd been through so recently. But I constantly ignored it and instead focused tirelessly on getting back to the old Andy as soon as humanly possible.

Yes, I was obsessive about my gym time, but it did help me regain my coordination, *and* the numbing had finally subsided so that I could type well enough to return to work. Spending time at the gym also got me out of the house enough to build confidence away from my seizure safety zone. The only thing I was afraid of more than a seizure itself was having one in public without Bruce. But it was time. I needed to take the uncomfortable step toward the real world. This would be the longest amount of time I had spent away from home and away from Bruce. A little extra makeup contouring, and you could hardly tell how much I resembled Quasimodo.

When I pulled up to my office building, there was a huge sign hanging from the roof that said, *Welcome Back, Andy!* I was equally embarrassed and grateful. I made up my mind. This was going to be a good day.

Brad, my stepdad *and* business partner, had taken care of everything while I was away and had still insisted on cutting me a paycheck during my absence. It was not lost on me how fortunate I was to have a family business, with decision makers who insisted I took my time to heal and a supportive staff who helped carry the weight of my absence.

Now it was time to do my part, even if my face was a little extra and I was anxious about all the seizure triggers in our tiny office. Miraculously, the day went smoothly (I only worked a half day—let's be real), and when all was said and done, I left feeling capable and fulfilled that I was able to contribute once again.

After I got the kids to bed, I slipped into the shower to enjoy the hot water and reflect on how far I'd come. My mind always wanders, and my thoughts are most alive when I'm alone in the steam. I was pretty dang proud that I had made it out alive, and with such motivation to thrive again.

Then I started rinsing my hair—still carefully, as my scar was only newly healed, with fresh pink skin.

But something didn't feel right. I jumped out of the shower to look in the mirror, and my fear was staring right back at me. My scar was opening up.

It's okay. It's okay. Maybe I scratched it in the shower. I will not freak out and call Jacki in a panic for a third time. It will be better in the morning. It will.

It was not better in the morning. My swelling had gone down, but what I'd hoped was a scratch was indeed my scar opening up. It wasn't really bleeding, but it wasn't scabbing either. Jacki told me that all signs pointed to an infection. Dr. Sanai would send an antibiotic prescription to my pharmacy, and I was to start taking it as soon as possible. If there was no improvement in a few days, I needed to call her back.

I tried to live the next few days as normally as possible. I basically ignored the reality of what was happening, until the same coach who'd helped me figure out how to lunge with a barbell and wouldn't let me quit a workout pointed it out to me.

"You're bleeding down your neck."

His face said it all. I thought he was going to faint! I played it off.

"Oh, that's okay. My scar is still healing."

I beelined for the bathroom, locked the door, and started crying at my reflection in the mirror. There was a trail of blood running down my neck, mixing with sweat from the workout I'd just finished. What was happening? The rest of my body wanted to heal, so why wouldn't this freaking scar?

I went home to wash my hair and clean out my incision. I was extra careful in the shower and combed my hair to part around the long trail of fresh skin. I sprayed Bactine on it in my own naive effort to help the situation. After the stinging subsided, I ran a cotton ball from the top of my incision to the bottom to help dry it out. I noticed every time I ran the cotton ball down my scar it would come back with more blood, but the blood was getting pinker and pinker. The soft spot under my incision was actually fluid that had begun oozing out of where it had opened.

Bruce was working, so I called my mom. She came over to see for herself. With her there, I decided to push a little harder.

"Oh my gosh."

If you've ever watched an abscess release on YouTube, you know what happened next. Piling up on my bathroom counter was cotton ball after cotton ball, topped with a salmon-pink-colored fluid similar to the consistency of Caladryl. It didn't smell, thank the Lord, but it wasn't straight-up blood either. My body was fighting an infection too close to my brain for comfort.

That was the slap in the face I needed to call Jacki back and let her know the antibiotics were not working. I left a message for her that night, and she called me back the next morning to set up an appointment for later that day.

When Bruce came home from work I told him that I needed to go back to see Dr. Sanai that afternoon. We were both deflated, but we wanted to make the best of it, so we stopped at Pita Jungle (I really do love that place) for a date of sorts on our way in.

My hair was still parted so that my incision could breathe, which made it necessary that I did everything humanly possible to keep the waitress on my good side. I felt like a disgusting freak, but I tried to make the best of this opportunity to have my favorite meal on the off chance I'd be admitted to the hospital again.

~~~

Jacki walked me back to a small exam room at Dr. Sanai's office. She put on some gloves and wasn't shy about flipping my hair around to examine every corner of that scar. Then she began to push firmly on it to see what happened. Even with all that had come out the day before, she got a little more.

"Uh, let me show this to Dr. Sanai."

She left the room to grab him. It was after hours, and he was wearing the day on his shoulders. Now here I sat with pink goo opening up his beautiful incision. I could see the disappointment in his face, but I knew it wasn't *about* me; it was *for* me. He knew what this meant I'd have to go through. I, on the other hand, did not.

He explained that I would need to go to the ER to get admitted so that he could wash out the incision tomorrow morning. *Sounds easy enough,* I thought to myself.

Then he explained what the procedure entailed. Reopening my skin, my skull, and my brain sack, looking for visible signs of infection close to the brain itself, then giving everything a thorough cleaning and rinsing, and finally, closing everything back up again.

Bruce and I sat there stunned.

"I have to do it again?"

I understood that it had to be done, but it felt like we'd just left. Apparently a brain infection is pretty serious.

Bruce lay in the ER bed with me late into the night, or maybe it was early morning; I can't exactly remember, but I do remember it was unusually quiet. We were quiet too, waiting for my room—and the storm. I eventually sent Bruce home so he could be with the kids when they woke up.

Not long after he left, I was taken to a no-frills room in a dark, empty part of the hospital. I had a small bed and antiseptic shampoo. I was to shower and wash my hair right away so that it could dry before surgery. The storm was in motion.

~~~

Bruce was running late getting the boys out the door that morning, and to top it off, surgery was scheduled for exactly the same time as rush-hour traffic.

My hair was sterile, and I was suited up in the good ol' backless gown. Everything was moving forward, but I wanted it to stop. Bruce wasn't there yet. There was no Clendon to calm my nerves either. In the nick of time, my mom showed up. I was so happy to see her, but I *needed* Bruce.

The nurse came over to raise my bed railings for the familiar journey down the hall.

"Okay, miss. Everyone is waiting for you."

I kept my eyes peeled to the entrance of the pre-op room, hoping for a glimpse of Bruce on my way back. Just as the nurse started to turn my bed around the corner, I saw him push himself through the doors.

As I made the turn, he looked at me and yelled, "I'm here!" He caught the nurse's attention, but she didn't stop. I felt horrible. The look on his face was despairing. All I could think about was him agonizing over his tardiness for the next however many hours this surgery was going to take. I couldn't wait for them to get to washing my brain so I could get to Bruce.

Waking up was a different experience this time. I woke up sad and defeated. My hair wasn't even braided. My head hurt. How had I not noticed this pain before?

Bruce walked around the curtain, smiling but with the same sadness I was feeling reflecting back in his eyes. We had been here not so long ago. Except this time there were no jokes or even smiles.

Back for my third tour in the Barrow ICU, the pain continued to get worse. I can't even describe it. I guess it's how you would imagine it feels if someone were to cut open your skull and mess around with your brain, then screw a plate in to hold everything together.

Whatever pain medication they gave me wasn't touching it, so they tried morphine. My body rejected it immediately and completely. First I couldn't tell which way was up. Then I started heaving uncontrollably. Nothing was coming up, but my body kept trying anyway. I remember the bottom of that trash can so vividly. The clear plastic bag covering the perfectly clean black canister. I was wishing for vomit so that my stomach would settle. My head was throbbing from the violent manner in which my body tried to rid itself of the morphine. A little something came up, and I lay back with tears behind my closed eyes, hoping to escape into sleep for a bit.

When I woke up, the ICU nurse checked the pad on my pillow. She freaked out. It was soaking wet. My new incision was leaking. A lot. She called for a doctor, and it was determined I needed a few additional stitches.

But here's the catch: they couldn't numb the area, for risk of further infection. More punctures equals more risk. Given my previous reaction to a strong painkiller, I was given a tiny white wafer that could have been a birth control pill for all I knew. It did nothing. A shot of tequila would have been more sufficient. But no time to smuggle in the good stuff; here comes the doc.

A young, handsome, overly confident white coat walked into my room without so much as eye contact as he took a phone call. While he was talking, my sweet nurse motioned for me to face her and lay on my side.

"Hold my hand," she whispered.

By the way she looked at me, I could tell this was going to be painful. He hung up and immediately went to work. I could hear his tray of instruments behind me. The occasional silence was suspenseful as I imagined him threading his hook. He never said a word to me, only formalities to the nurse. He put one hand on my head, pressing it into my pillow. I held onto my nurse even tighter.

Eyes closed and pulling her hand deeper into my chest, I felt *everything*. Every puncture, every strand of thread running through my skin, every knot, every tight pull, over and over again. At first I was quiet, but eventually I lost my composure. Sobs escaped me as I lay there in the fetal position. I was as helpless as a baby in that moment. All I could do was surrender to it.

When the doctor was done he nonchalantly snapped off his gloves and left the room. I cried hard, and the nurse motioned for a stunned Bruce to come over and take her position while she cleaned up. Everyone was silent. All that could be heard was my cry of forfeit. Just hours after surgery, and I was already giving up without a shred of strength to fight.

After that, I became numb to how anything I did could make a difference. I simply did as I was told. *Be good, and maybe I'll make it out of here eventually.* That was my mentality. So when they told me it was time to try and walk, I did, but not because I wanted to.

The best part about walking in ICU are the glass walls. You can see everything. The worst part about walking in ICU are the glass walls. You can see everything.

I noticed the girl just next door to me was hooked up to a bunch of machines, unresponsive. Her room was full with family and friends. She didn't look any older than sixteen. Everyone was crying. I overheard something about a car accident.

All I had ever wanted on this journey was enough time to raise my kids, and as I paused there in front of her room, I watched her parents live out their worst nightmare. And the girl? She might never even get the privilege to know what having a family of her own felt like. "Why, God?" I felt angry that He put all of us through this.

I walked one more lap. Seeing that girl and her family any more than that would have been too much. Back in my room I opted for a chair instead of the bed. As soon as I settled in I saw Julia through the glass wall, walking down the hall with a big smile.

She walked right in and started to compliment me for being out of bed, but before she could finish I interrupted: "Go home. I have nothing good to say."

"Probably because you look like a mess. Just because you feel like crap doesn't mean you have to look like it." All this was coming out of her mouth as she combed my hair with her fingers and proceeded to braid it. Just like that, my pity party was over.

Eventually I made it back to the recovery floor with my new constant companion, an IV of antibiotics. The first night on the floor I started to panic. I couldn't handle the hospital for one second longer. I was crying and crying, and the tears just wouldn't stop. I was on a four-hour bag of antibiotics, so I couldn't go outside. It was 2 a.m. anyway, and the nurse wasn't keen on the idea. But I was relentless. I guess I did have a little fight in me after all.

She didn't let me go outside, but she escorted us to a "meditation room" or something of that sort down the hall. It had the kind of music playing you would hear when getting a massage or facial ... wooden flutes or whatever. I was not impressed. This was the most corporate-looking "meditation room" I had ever seen. Chairs in rows and plastic plants! *Are you kidding me?!*

I walked over to the water wall. I put my hand on it, expecting the water to be running behind the glass, but it hit my fingers. I started crying again. Bruce helped me down to the floor, where I collapsed in my tears, still pressing my hand against the wall. Finally, something real. I stayed in that posture until my face was dry. Bruce sat in one of the chairs, tired and helpless. I realized he was going through this too.

I released my pruning hand from the wall and crawled over to his feet. After I wrapped myself around him, we sat there in silence for the next hour or so. Perhaps we even unintentionally meditated.

About the exact same time my IV pole started beeping to let us know that it was finished, my nurse came in. She said she could postpone the next IV for fifteen minutes if I wanted to take a walk outside in the healing garden downstairs. I did want that—so desperately.

It was dark, and the air was hot on my skin, with temperatures still near one hundred degrees at night. That's an Arizona summer for you. Looking up I could see a few stars, even through the city lights. Bruce held my hand as we walked the paths. A big palo verde tree caught my attention. I don't know what came over me, but I was compelled to listen to it. I felt bad for the tree—that it was planted in the middle of the city, surrounded by concrete and tall buildings.

I bet no one listens to what the tree *wants. They're holding it hostage! Just like me.*

Yes, I was extremely tired and fatigued. I was fully aware that I was not in my right mind, but I explored these thoughts anyway. Maybe this level of crazy was a defense tactic my mind was using to keep me from *completely* losing it.

I pressed my ear to the tree trunk and put my arms around it. I bet this tree never had a hug or anyone to listen. I could hear a trickle in the trunk, or maybe it was my imagination, but I felt a deep connection. I don't know why or how, but my energy became lighter.

I asked Bruce if he wanted to listen, and he respectfully declined. He's always been the reasonable one. Instead he reminded me, "It's time to go back for your next IV bag."

Ugh.

12. PLAYING CATCHUP

Healing isn't always graceful, but it's still beautiful.

As I woke up from only a few hours of sleep, a squeaky-shoed nurse took unnecessarily short steps into my room and around the curtain. "Gooood morning, Mrs. Ptaaaaaacek," he said in a voice that trailed up into a high pitch. He ran the usual bilateral strength tests, asked me to follow his finger with my eyes, etc., etc., and then he went on to incessantly question me about my poop... thoroughly disappointed that I hadn't gone yet. *He* was disappointed in *me*.

I was disappointed in me! I didn't need anyone else chiming in about what I should be better at. Pooping was at the bottom of my priority list, but it was at the top of his. It's all he wanted to talk about. You see, I'm a recovering people pleaser. I *wanted* to poop for him, but he was constantly reminded me of my inadequacy as a pooper, and thus my resentment was escalating.

I'll admit that my temperament had flipped a switch this time around, but if he came in with those squeaky shoes, singing my name and asking me about my poop one more time, I was going to throw something at him. I was serious. Bruce knew I was serious too.

"Andy, you can't throw things at nurses—they'll tie you to your bed."

The things we never thought we'd say.

Realizing my claustrophobia was more of a threat than his squeaky shoes and poop interrogations, I kept my temper under control on the outside. But on the inside, I was o-v-e-r it. Looking back, I can see that I was taking out my frustration about my circumstance on him. He was a completely delightful person (even if he did have squeaky shoes), but for the entirety of his twelve-hour shift, I mostly fantasized about unleashing my pent-up anger on him.

Besides pooping, I needed to get a PICC line before I was allowed to go home. A PICC (peripherally inserted central catheter) line is like a permanent IV that makes it easy to connect and disconnect to intravenous antibiotics. I was fine with it if it meant I was one step closer to going home—until they asked me which arm I could basically go without using for the next three months. Apparently you aren't supposed to lift anything more than ten pounds with the arm a PICC line is in. No picking up kids, barbells, or even grocery bags. All that progress I had made—gone. I'd have to start over.

I was leaving the hospital on a sour note, but I was leaving. As part of my discharge instructions I was given all kinds of information about my new "friend" in my arm. They let me know I'd be set up with a home-health nurse who would teach me how to give myself IVs at home and check my arm weekly. "She better not have squeaky shoes," was my response.

She didn't. In fact, she was the sweetest lady you'd ever be lucky enough to meet. She taught me exactly how to use the PICC line and even gave me some pro tips. On the other hand, the actual antibiotics were not agreeing with me. The hospital antibiotics were too harsh to take long term, but as we tried different options, I'd get the forewarned life-threatening side effects every single time. Finding the right antibiotic was scary and tricky. Eventually I settled for lizard skin and acne as the side effect of choice. I took it one day at a time. Three months was too far away.

Meanwhile, Brad designed these amazing *Andy's Army* T-shirts that my gym sponsored. They were working on this idea behind my back, and when I found out I was completely embarrassed per usual at the attention, but I was also completely humbled. There was an image on the back of the shirt of fists in the air, wearing the bracelets I gave everyone. Hundreds of shirts were sold, and because we had great insurance that didn't put much of a financial strain on us, we split the profits between my surgeon's research center, PICC line covers for my home-health nurse to give to her other patients (the ones they send you home with are not comfortable or discrete), and the application process to receive medical cannabis for seizure and cancer prevention (more on this later).

Thank God for my people. Just when I started recoiling and slumping into the black hole of depression, they shined a light on me with their continued support. They were rooting for me. I needed to figure out how to give them something to root for.

~~~

I received a text from Julia that she wanted to grab a tea with me. I was home alone that day while Bruce was at work and both the kids were at school. When she knocked on the front door, I was sitting in my silent, dark living room for another antibiotic infusion—my new normal. I carried my IV pole to the door and let her in.

"What is going on in this house?!" she asked as she walked right past me and went to work opening all the blinds. "It's so depressing in here."

I carried my IV pole back to the recliner.

"You don't take your IVs like this all the time, do you?"

I did—and she was making me quite aware that I was allowing myself to sink deeper and deeper into depression with every IV. I agreed to stop this sad ritual from now on. Instead of sitting alone in the dark, I would let light in, read, talk to someone, or do whatever, as long as I wasn't shutting myself off when I turned the IV on.

When the infusion finished I disconnected the bag and did all the fancy stuff the home-health nurse had taught me. Jules was impressed with my IV skills, which made me feel good, her being a trauma nurse and all.

I was finished and ready to go, but not really. I was anxious to leave the house. If I wanted this to be a positive experience, I had to ignore my irrational fear that everyone was going to stare at my PICC line and whisper to each other with speculations about what my illness could be.

The thing is, I *knew* this was irrational, but it twisted me up inside. I had never gone through this before. I didn't know what the road to recovery looked like, so I did a little too much looking outward than inward to gauge my progress. By putting so much weight on the reactions of others, I became paranoid that people weren't being honest with me about what they were really thinking. I started to feel like even my family had secret conversations behind my back about planning my funeral, how they would raise my kids and move on without me. Everyone except Bruce and Julia was always so delicate with me, which made me suspicious. Behind all the positivity and careful words, what were they really thinking?

Going for tea with Julia was good for me. She's no nonsense. If you tell her something is one way she'll make you question why it's not the other. In her mind, if you're going to feel deeply about something you'd better have it figured out from all angles. I didn't, and she poked holes in *all* my conspiracy theories.

By the end of our tea date, no one had asked about my arm. I don't even think anyone really noticed. Back at my house, I gave Jules a big hug before stepping out of the car. For the first time in a long time I felt somewhat normal.

~~~

Like a ton of bricks it hit me: "Bruce is at work." The mere thought of him in possible danger sucked the wind out of me. Over the years I had gotten comfortable with his job, but I had almost forgotten what *work* was for him. It was pulling people out of car accidents on busy roads, it was welfare checks on passed-out drunk people with weapons, it was *running into burning buildings*.

"What. The. Hell. He is going to die today. If he dies the kids have no hope, because I don't even know if my brain is going to make it through this infection, and even if it does the cancer will probably come back and I'll die, and my poor kids! I'm the worst mom ever. What was I thinking having kids if we were just going to die on them! Plus, I'm supposed to die first. If Bruce dies first I will certainly fall apart without him. How am I supposed to honor his life when I can't hold mine together? He is the *glue* holding us together. We'll all fall apart without him. If he dies I will lose my mind for real, and if I don't die from the infection or cancer, I may as well have because I'll be crazy, and my kids will be even more damaged taking care of a crazy mom who blankly stares at the wall than one who died young on a good note. Lord, don't let him die!"

Right then a rush came over my body, almost the same rush I'd felt when I had seizures.

"No. No. No," I told myself as I ran to the middle of the living room carpet and sat down. "Do not have a seizure."

The seconds passed, and the seizure didn't come, but the feeling never went away. In a powerful release, my welled-up eyes let go, and I started bawling right there, in the middle of the living room. Morbid thoughts were spiraling around me louder and louder. My heart was racing, and I wanted to run away, but to where? Jacki. She'd had all the answers before. I knew my mind was not right; maybe she'd experienced this before in other patients.

I pulled myself together enough to make the call, but as soon as I heard her voice mine fell apart while I tried to explain what I was going through.

"It sounds pretty bad right now; do you have any clonazepam?"

Confused, I answered, "Yes, but the seizure never came."

"You're not going to have a seizure. You're having a panic attack."

I remembered that the prescribing doctor had told me that clonazepam can be used for panic attacks as well.

Jacki told me to take the clonazepam as soon as we got off the phone and then to follow up with my new neurologist and maybe even a support group through the Gray Matters Foundation or a therapist to talk through everything with. I wanted to see Dr. Sanai because he knew me and the facts about my medical situation, but she reminded me that he was a surgeon and that not having to see him was a good thing.

So I sat on the couch with my tiny dose of clonazepam and let it melt under my tongue. A new rush came over my body. It was a heavy calming feeling, like a long hug from the universe.

~~~

When Bruce came home the next morning I hugged him and told him not to die.

"I need you to be extra careful—at all costs," I told him sternly. "This is serious. If you die, I will die by osmosis, or at least my mind will. The possibility that this could happen is tearing me up."

As ridiculous as it was, I made him promise me that he wouldn't die. Obviously he had no control over that, but I made him promise me he would put his own safety above others. That he'd play every call *safe*. I believed him when he promised me, but looking back and knowing who he is, I guarantee he did nothing of the sort.

When he wasn't at work trying not to die, Bruce and I went on frequent walks to ease my new friend, anxiety. For me, when I'm anxious I'm also antsy. Walking helps equalize my mind with my body.

On one such walk, I couldn't help but notice the neighborhood we were walking in was never one that we'd wanted to live in. I mean, I loved the lake, but the houses were so close together we may as well have been sharing walls, and the yards were so tiny the kids did a lot of their playing in the street with me out there yelling, "Car!" every thirty seconds.

Circumstance had brought us here, and we were grateful to be out of the trailer, but right before all of this had happened, we were finally searching for the forever home we'd worked so hard to save for. We had been so excited to take on that new chapter, until God flipped the script. Now it just didn't seem right. We were in no condition to make any big life decisions. We were barely hanging on to our current life situation.

While our conversation circled around this perfectly logical reasoning to eventually move onto our forever home, I had to confess my deepest, most dispiriting reasoning to Bruce: "I'm afraid I might not make it to our *forever*."

It was honest and raw and extremely hard for me to say out loud, but at the time it felt as though we'd be picking out a home for them, not us. At the very least, I was sane enough to realize that looking for forever homes was not a healthy situation to put myself through or to subject Bruce to.

We agreed to stay in the rental, but Bruce made it clear that it was not because of my reasoning. Whatever the reason, I felt a little lighter after that walk.

My relationship with Bruce during this time remained tender. I asked a lot of him with all of my breakdowns and spiraling anxiety, but he never looked at me like I was any different. He never talked to or treated me like I was fragile either. To him, I was the same girl now that he'd always loved. But honest to God, when he kissed my head just like he always used to do, my heart broke every single time. My head. The proof of my damage. I would immediately turn inward, feeling unworthy of affection because being with him now was just going to make it harder on him when I was not.

On one such occasion, we were lying in bed, and he wrapped his arms around me, pulling me into his chest to give me a kiss. His kiss landed on the side of my head—the same side that was dented and scarred and was the source of so much pain in our lives. He reached for my face to kiss my lips next, but he felt my tears.

"I'm sorry," I told him.

But he wouldn't hear those words. He sat up abruptly, and I slid up to lean against the headboard. He wanted to talk through it all. This is totally Bruce's style of communication. He needs to fix everything on the spot. I explained to him how I felt damaged. How I knew I was dying faster than him, than anyone else I knew.

"Stop it." I was surprised how adamant he was about this, but he kept going. "You do not know you are dying faster. Perfectly healthy people die in car accidents every day. I see them at work. You die when you die, and there's nothing you can do about it. I love you, and I don't give a shit about your scar or your dented head."

Wow. Talk about yanking someone out of a pity party. Everything he said was true, and it started the process of chipping away at the victim mindset I had started buying into. So what if my head was a mess and I had lines coming out of my arms and a fanny pack full of IV antibiotics? *It is what it is.* I felt less sorry for myself, but I had to direct all this energy somewhere.

Instead of focusing on what I was going through, I started to wonder what all the people around me were going through. I would watch people and the energy they projected. They were living, smiling and thriving even, but everyone has their things. I would imagine what demons they were battling on the inside while their outside looked so put-together. A miscarriage. An affair. A divorce. A sick parent. An assault. A cancer growing they didn't even know about yet. This was a blessing and a curse. As I became more empathetic to the imaginary adversities of others, I started to feel *too* much. Now instead of being consumed by my own things, I would take on the fear and uncertainty of whatever anyone else was hypothetically going through—real or not.

My emotions ran rampant, and anxiety dug its claws a little deeper. I wasn't quite aware how it was taking hold—I just thought these feelings of fear were part of processing everything. I believed the more time that accrued between then and now would prove that I was healing, and the less afraid I would be. Or so I hoped.

Part of proving to myself that I was healing was seeing physical progress. I equated improvements in stamina and strength with my overall health, believing that through working out, the old Andy—the healthy Andy—would be back, and cancer would disappear from my world like it never even existed.

This time, the progress was much slower, and the reality of that made getting out of bed and moving my body much harder than before. I wasn't ready for the gym this time. I wasn't ready for the people either, but I did need to try *something*.

Bruce took me to the Glendale Community College track to walk, run, and climb bleachers. I knew I could walk, but running might end with me in a heap of road rash on the ground.

When we walked through the gates I saw a silver-haired man running the track like nobody's business. I envied him. He had lived long enough to get silver hair, *and* he was running like a boss. He ran laps around me—at first.

We started out slowly, just getting my bearings. Then Bruce challenged me to run the straights and walk the turns. He stayed right there by my side.

Run, walk, run, walk, until we had made it to the last straightaway, and he declared, "We're running hard this time! Finish strong!"

I actually pushed myself. I didn't go through the motions like I had up until that moment. I didn't care if I fell down. I didn't care if that old man passed me. I ran like I was giving death, doubt, pain, and fear the middle finger.

This got Bruce excited to see what else I could do. As we made our way to our water bottles in the shade under the bleachers, he looked up and asked if I wanted to go to the top. I looked up too. Then closer, at the many big steps. "That's gonna hurt."

He grinned like I was talking about leg gains, but I was talking about falling down the bleachers. He took one more drink from his water bottle. "Okay, let's go."

I reluctantly followed him. I was legit scared and overwhelmed. As we started climbing, I told myself, "One foot at a time. Focus on *just* the step I'm on."

Meanwhile Bruce started sprinting up to the top, skipping steps with his long legs. "Oh, God, he's going to make me run too."

But he knew better. He knew he didn't have to ask or even tell me to sprint. He just needed to dangle the possibility in front of me. He knows my competitive spirit runs deep, and it was still somewhere in there.

I started climbing a little faster. He was already on his way back down. Then I heard his fast steps get louder behind me. He was on his way up again. I tried to run a little, but fear took over, spiraling one what-if into the next. *What if I lose balance and fall down these bleachers? What if I crack my head open? What if the ambulance has no idea what to do with my brain situation? What if I never even make it to the hospital before my brain swells up or bleeds out?*

Oh gosh, Andy. *Shut up.* An internal battle was waged.

What if none *of that happens? What about when you were in high school and jumped off all those cliffs at Lake Pleasant? Or that huge one at Lake Powell?* A lot could have gone wrong—but it hadn't. *What about that time you should have died pretending you were the chick from* The Fast and the Furious *in your blue Ford Taurus, stealing toilet paper for an epic night of teepee wars? Remember all the times you wrecked that car? If you can live through that, you can certainly live though a few fast steps on the bleachers.*

Here comes Bruce on his way down again, looking a little tired. Maybe tired enough that I'll be able to hang with him on his way back up. I heard his steps behind me again. *Okay, Andy. Here we go.* I picked up the pace, and I just went for it. One step at a time, I brought my knee up and pushed off hard with the other foot. Over and over again, until I was standing at the top of the bleachers, holding onto the chain-link fence, breathing hard and looking out at the campus, my old stomping grounds before ASU. It was here that this guy named Chris cheated off my microeconomics tests and eventually introduced me to his friend, Bruce, the guy standing with me right this second. I looked over at him, and he smiled at me. "I knew you could do it."

I wanted more of this feeling.

Since I still had a PICC line, I couldn't do any lifting, but I could *wear* weight. A while back I had tested a female body-armor prototype for TYR Tactical. They were making a new XS-sized vest based on my build, and it was so fun to be part of the development process. They took my measurements at their ginormous warehouse, where I got to meet all the people who would be involved in creating the prototype. Just a couple weeks later I wore the vest for a workout of running, push-ups, squats, and pull-ups. Jane, one of the owners (and one of the coolest people you'll ever meet), took pictures and video of the vest in action, then inspected my body for any rub marks and the vest for any defects. I specifically remembered how much harder the running and squats were. *I wonder if they're done with the prototype? I wonder if they'll let me buy it? I mean, I've already sweated in it—maybe it's smelly and they want to get rid of it anyway?* So I got in touch with Jane, and she *gave* me a new one. What?! I was beyond excited.

I wore that vest for hours at a time in the gym, jerry-rigging additional iron plates inside the armor compartment. I ran, did box step-ups, squats, lunges, kettlebell work, anything and everything that didn't involve my left arm. I was developing an obsession with fitness like never before, dreaming about the day my arm would be free and I could do it all. I promised myself I wouldn't whine about tough workouts in the future. In those moments I would remember how badly I wanted to do it *now* and embrace the privilege to suck wind and feel my body freak out under heavy loads when I am able.

After a month or so of working out in the corner, it was time for me to return to coaching. I was still having so much anxiety, and I dreaded the energy it would take to chipper up and pretend to be myself. Consequently, the first workout I came back to coach was the same day we hosted a special breast cancer awareness workout at our gym with Barbells for Boobs, a prominent nonprofit in the fitness community.

When I spoke, you could hear a pin drop in the middle of that huge gym—usually filled with side banter and people prematurely claiming their equipment. Everyone was intently hanging on to my every word as I explained the significance of the workout and the movements, a far cry from what I was used to. I could feel their curiosity overshadowing whatever was coming out of my mouth. They weren't listening to my words but to my posture, my nonverbals, my eyes, trying to read between the lines. It was a heavy moment, and while they were silently wondering what was going on with me, I looked right back at them, wondering the same. *Who else in this room has been affected by cancer? Who else in this room* will get *cancer?* It was inevitable that someone had and someone would. It broke my heart.

My voice started to waver, so I introduced the short promo video to get the class pumped to be part of this great cause. As it played, I disengaged from the video message in an effort to pull myself together. I kept repeating to myself, "Do not cry on your first day back."

~~~

My PICC line was finally scheduled to be removed the day after Halloween. We celebrated the eve with our traditional driveway bonfire, chili, cornbread, and all-you-can-eat candy. This was the close of a long, hard chapter in our lives. I was excited to finally be able to find the old Andy somewhere in that gym she used to thrive in.

I immediately started CrossFitting again, supplementing additional strength work and then completely transitioning to weightlifting. This had always been the intention, from the time I realized I could hook-grip after surgery, and now I was finally ready to chase that goal. I would compete at a local meet exactly one year after surgery, where I would qualify to compete at the national level. But what started out as a fulfilling version of physical and mental "therapy" had somehow morphed into an unhealthy obsession as I started training for the big meet.

I had serendipitously acquired a legit coach who had actually *won* his weight class at the American Open and had more medals than he could count. Brian Reisenauer poured a lot into my new goals. He believed in me, and that helped me believe in myself. But when I underperformed I had legit meltdowns. Every time my strength peaked, I felt unstoppable. Every time it fell below my standards, I fell apart. Brian helped me understand that I had created an unrealistic correlation between my progress in the gym and my progress in healing. That inaccurate mindset eventually overshadowed *everything* in my life. Everything came second to the gym. To me, the gym was keeping me alive, and what was the point of everything else if I wasn't alive?

Initially this mindset stunted my healing and I was falling into a very dark place. Dealing with small challenges was hard at this point, so when Christmas rolled around, I pretty much gave up before I even tried. I didn't want to decorate, shop, or even get a tree. When had Christmas become such a production? I was vetoed when I suggested to our families that we skip the gifts this year and write heartfelt notes to each other instead.

As the lights started going up around the city, the boys got that magic twinkle in their eyes, and no matter how much I didn't want to, I finally pulled out the Christmas decorations, with Bruce's help. He really came through that year. It's a holiday that mostly falls on my lap, but there he was, picking out gifts and loading up the family to pick out a tree.

Gosh, I remember that night like it was yesterday. It wasn't fancy. We didn't go to one of those adorable tree lots with the holiday ambiance and endless choices. We went to the neighborhood Lowe's, and the kids picked out a tree they named Fluffy. I was so over it. *They want* how much *for a dying tree?* How bizarre is Christmas?! We buy trees, not even the ones we can plant later, to put in our house, so Santa can put presents under it? What a weird and wasteful birthday celebration for Jesus. I was Scrooging so hard when the kids caught the corner of my eye. They were all giggles and smiles. The man wrapping up our tree had given them the bottom slice of the stump, and they were throwing it back and forth.

Bruce carried the tree to the truck and tasked the boys with holding it upright while he moved some things around. Still sort of detached from the situation, I didn't help or intervene. I stood back and watched them try to keep the tree from falling over with squeals of excitement. I was witnessing the Christmas spirit. This is why we do these crazy things for Jesus's birthday: for that feeling of joy that comes with doing something out of the ordinary. I broke a smile at this simple moment, and my heart grew ten sizes that day. Wait, now I'm getting *Scrooge* and *The Grinch* mixed up. Either way, I got over myself enough to see what was true, just in time for Christmas.

Even though the family didn't want to forgo gifts for notes, I wrote one to Bruce anyway and left it on his pillow. I peeked around the corner when I noticed him finding it. He sat down on the side of our bed to read it. I watched his back start to shake and his head fall. He was crying. I *did not* mean for that! The man never cries, but with all the weight he had been carrying, I guess the release was necessary. When I walked in, he turned to me and pulled me in tight.

> Bruce,
>
> Thank you for carrying the Christmas spirit for the both of us. I thought I'd have more, but I guess I'm still catching up a bit. You've been such a rock for me this year, and you've been a real example of unconditional love. I don't know how you did it sometimes. You're always in my prayers—thanking God for the man you are to our family. I'm looking forward to a *NEW* year with you and many more *Merry* Christmases. I love you beyond words.
>
> XO
>
> Andy

Thank you, Christmas.

13. SO THIS IS THIRTY-THREE

How we respond is the only thing we can really control.

Once a month I would get blood drawn, and then Bruce and I would make the drive downtown to the infectious disease doctor for his official interpretation. Sitting in the waiting room were people either double my age or very visibly sick. *These* had become my people, but it was still a little shocking to me every time I stepped off the elevator directly into the waiting room with them. For the past few months I had been grouped with people on life support or in cages, and now the chronically ill.

"We don't belong here," Bruce said on my first visit back since getting the PICC line removed.

"Shhh." He's always embarrassing me with his loudness. Working on the fire truck has definitely taken a toll on his ears. When he thinks he's whispering, well, he's not. Proof we *should* be here—pretty much everyone has hearing aids, and *he* needs one!

But it got me thinking. *Maybe these aren't my people. Maybe I'm not chronically ill. Maybe today the doc will say I'm free to go live my life antibiotic-free with a happy tummy and great skin!*

Back in the exam room, on crinkly white paper, the doctor briefly looked at my scar, as always, to make sure it wasn't agitated. He was an awkward, quiet guy, but he was always in a good mood. Bruce made a game out of trying to get him to laugh at every appointment. He had the best laugh, and it made *us* laugh. For such a quiet and serious person, the big sharp noise Bruce was able to provoke out of his small body was always the highlight of the dreaded visit.

He was in approval of my bloodwork, but I would not be antibiotic-free. Instead I would continue with oral antibiotics and instructions to continue checking in monthly with more bloodwork. At every visit, I'd confirm the goal date to quit, and when the day finally came around, it was pushed back. The situation was becoming disheartening, but finally, nearing my thirty-third birthday, my white blood cells showed up, and I was released from the pills, the monthly check-ins, and the depressing waiting room.

What was shaping up to be the best birthday ever suddenly took quite a turn. The dreaded rush came over my body. It wasn't a panic attack. In a matter of seconds, my left arm started to shake involuntarily, and when it was over, my hand was limp. The same cycle happened three times. My hand, in a postictal state, had stopped working altogether. I was bawling like a child, terrified that the cancer was back, or the infection. Would my hand stay like this?! Bruce was sitting on the edge of the bed with me, rubbing my arm and hand. I couldn't feel it. My face was soaked with tears and snot. I got up to wash my face and grabbed for the handle to turn on the water, but my hand slid right off it. Determined and somewhat out of my mind, I turned the water on by pushing the handle with the top of my hand before I realized I could use the other one. I used my right hand to rinse my face, and as I was drying it, I looked down at my curled-in left hand. "Please work."

Although I couldn't make a fist, I was able to sort of pinch my thumb and the rest of my stiff fingers together. I tried grasping the towel with my crab hand and was able to hold it. Realizing my hand was starting to function again, I started to calm down. Bruce took the initiative to call Jacki again as I stressed over what could be wrong.

She sent us to the hospital for a scan to be on the safe side.

I had just recently had my first follow-up scan. My neurologist had been pleased and had told us that everything looked stable. I kept hearing her words: "You'd be surprised at how much of your brain you can live without!" Like living with a hole in your brain was completely normal. That visit was actually the first time I saw my post-surgery scans. Knowing is one thing, but seeing is completely different. She was enthralled with showing me every angle. I pretended to geek out with her, but inside I was knotting up. I was really missing part of myself, and that part of me had been sent to be poked and prodded by researchers in a lab somewhere after surgery. I think Dr. Sanai had even told me my tumor would be frozen in case I had a recurrence and they needed to test treatment options. It all felt a little *Hannibal Lecter*.

But now I was remembering her words in a positive light, "You'd be surprised at how much of your brain you can live without." I was also drawing my attention to the present moment. *I'm here. I'm breathing. I can think. I'm alive. I'm okay.*

After a million hours we were told everything looked fine. The doctor didn't really have a solid explanation, but in my mind I was imagining my brain trying to make new pathways around the giant hole. It was just a little crash. *My body can do this. It will find a new way.*

Bruce and I were beyond relieved, and I was even given an early birthday gift—new seizure medication.

A considerable amount of time after this incident, I was allowed to start weaning down on the dosage, all the while remaining seizure-free. I choose to do this because the medications had the worst side effects and made me feel less like myself than I felt comfortable with on a daily basis.

Even though seizures are about the scariest thing I can imagine, I was gaining confidence that my days of uncontrollable convulsions were officially behind me.

My heart was feeling lighter, and my mood was less stressed than ever. This was the road to recovery I'd been trying to find. I wasn't lost anymore. I just had to stay the course.

~~~

In my world, there's not a lot that tops spending the afternoon being creative at work, then coming home to Bruce's homemade spaghetti sauce on the stove while happy kids play dinosaurs.

I put my stuff down and walked straight to the kitchen for a sample. Bruce caught me.

"Get out of there! It's not done!"

I smiled in his direction, and as I attempted to lick the sauce off my finger, I missed and hit my cheek instead.

"Oh my gosh, that's weird!"

Not thinking much of it, I started walking his way to give him a hug.

As I pressed my head against his chest I realized, "I'm going to have a seizure."

He didn't believe it.

"No, you're not."

Right there in his arms I felt a rush beyond anything else I had experienced before. My eyes had already started welling up as I untangled myself from him and started running for the bedroom so the kids wouldn't see me.

He followed after me—still not convinced this was really happening—but I never made it to the bedroom. My arm flew up, and my legs gave out. The last thing I remember is Bruce breaking my fall and the carpet on my cheek. It was the big one. A total blackout.

I woke up propped against the doorjamb, with my kids' heads peeking over the couch at me. Bruce asked me some questions, but I couldn't find my voice. Then he asked me if I knew their names, pointing at our kids. I knew them. I knew I loved them. I stared into their big eyes trying to bring their names to my mouth, and I just couldn't. My heart broke hard. I didn't know my kids' names.

Bruce helped me get up and walked me the rest of the way to our bed and tucked me in to rest. Exhausted, I dozed off. Or so I thought. I never really fell asleep. I was in and out of consciousness as my mind tried to wake up or reboot or whatever it does.

Lying there, I heard my mom's voice. *What's she doing here?* I heard her voice get closer to my room. As she walked in I turned over and smiled at her, feeling happy and extremely refreshed, like I had just taken a three-hour nap.

"What are you doing here?"

"You just had a seizure, and I wanted to check on you." Bruce had called her to let her know what happened, and she had rushed over. "Do you know my name?"

"You're my mom." But her name wasn't really available to me yet. "Seizure? Why would I have a seizure? I was just taking a nap."

Or so I thought. I was feeling happy-go-lucky and confused by all the attention.

Bruce was standing there with a serious look on his face, nodding his head. "You had a seizure."

Just like that my heart sank, and the happiness was sucked out of me. I remembered. I'd had brain surgery... because I had brain cancer... now I get seizures. I was struck by sadness. It was like finding out all over again.

"I forgot my kids' names," I confessed to my mom.

"But you know them now?"

I hoped so. Let's see what comes out...

"Tavin and Grant?"

I remembered, all right. I remembered that I was still broken. No matter how much time had passed or how good things seemed to be going I would always have a hole in my brain screwing things up.

My remarkable recovery wasn't so remarkable anymore. Coming to terms with my mortality became overwhelming. I started having excessive panic attacks and anxiety. It got to the point that even hearing the leaves on a tree startled me. Panic attacks would come in waves, over and over again. I got good at talking myself down once I knew how to recognize the difference between a panic attack and the aura I felt before a seizure.

In my mind I knew the steps, and I knew the logic, but my body would not cooperate. My body was in constant fight-or-flight, which made being in public overstimulating and trying to sleep impossible. If I had lived in an uncivilized tribe, I would have totally been the hardest to kill. I was in constant survival mode, aware of every little thing happening around me as though it were happening in slow motion and extra loud. While the outside world was intense, my mind was more so. Racing thoughts took on their own life and could not be reined in. Just like my body was acting out with panic attacks, my mind would find and show me things I didn't want to think about.

Not able to sleep, I would pace the house, moving from room to room, hoping the new environment would help me calm down and find sleep. I'd start out in my own room, then move to my kids' room, then to the couch with a podcast or something soothing in my headphones to drown out the incessant self-talk.

I tried guided meditation apps, and I even tried melatonin, but my body would physically fight rest. As soon as I felt the heaviness of the melatonin, my body reacted with a panic attack. The smallest feeling of being out of control sent my mind into panic mode. Even if I did doze off, my body would jerk itself awake. Sometimes I would see visions of the operating room or my opening wound when jolting awake. I realized I was unconsciously correlating going to sleep with going under the knife. I was also correlating sleeping meds with the dreaded hospital meds, and my body was in full-on protest.

But let's be real now; I needed to sleep. I was starting to feel drunk, crazy, or both. Maybe I needed to skip the melatonin and go for something that *forced* me asleep. I had a medical marijuana card that I used to get full-extract CBD-oil capsules. The CBD strain I took was nonpsychoactive (I could write another book about the amazing benefits of full-extract CBD, including seizure brain cancer management), but on one particular visit to the dispensary, I asked about the oil capsules with THC. I learned that indica-strain capsules produced a body-relaxation high. Everything they said sounded like everything I needed. I had never been high before (minus the hospital drugs of course), but at this point in my sleep deprivation, I already felt like a character in *Alice in Wonderland*. If I wanted to make it back to the real world, I *needed* sleep, and I was willing to do whatever it took to get it.

That night I took a 20 mg indica-oil pill in place of my CBD-oil pill. I was so excited to crawl into bed in anticipation of a solid night of sleep. A few hours later I woke up to pee. But my body was a gazillion pounds, and my mattress was *swallowing* me. By the grace of God I rolled out of bed and stumbled to the bathroom. Sitting on the toilet, I realized, *I'm so freaking high.* Now the toilet was swallowing me! I coached myself though the basic functions of potty training and walked the ten miles back to bed.

When I lay down, my arm became pinched under me. Operation Free My Arm had commenced. Bruce woke up in the commotion.

"I need your help!"

Startled, he sat up and turned the light on.

"Lift my body up, I can't free my arm!"

He helped me sit up, and it took everything I had to lift my hand up in front of my face.

"Why is my hand so far away?!"

I was legit panicking. Bruce was legit laughing.

"Abort! Call 911! This is going wrong!"

"Andy, I am 911. You'll have to let it take its course."

"Well, give me an IV! I need to flush this out of my system!"

"Andy, mind over matter. Don't make this a bad experience. Try to embrace it."

What the hell?! Is he serious?! I'm dying!

"Well, turn the lights off then, if you're not going to help me—I can't see all the weirdness."

Bruce was full-on sleeping in less than five minutes. Meanwhile, I was watching the air move—in the dark. I forced my eyes shut and tried to focus on relaxing, but I was still seeing things behind my eyelids. *Is this a portal to the end of the universe? Andy, stop. No thinking.* So I just watched the end of the universe expand behind my eyelids and miraculously fell asleep. It was the hardest I had slept in a long time. But I was still high in the morning. Never again.

14. DON'T CALL ME A SURVIVOR

God can make all things new. And he does.

The first time I was called a "survivor," I felt sick. In that one word, I officially lost the person I used to be. I had become tainted by cancer. And to make it worse, the label implied that the battle was won. It was not. "Survivor," to me, felt like a cop-out. A label put on me to make the world feel better about my situation. Like, "Andy's just fine; she's a survivor." Little did anyone know, I was *barely* surviving. It had not been accomplished, nor would it ever be accomplished. I knew this because I was sentenced to scans every six months for twenty years, or for as long as I lived, whichever came first. If I make it twenty years, I will be fifty-two.

For those of us who battle cancer or a trauma, we carry it with us always. It's not enough to simply survive it, but we must learn how to thrive *despite* it.

I realize fifty-two years old is a short life expectancy for a best-case scenario, but when you go from "might not be able to raise your kids" to "might be a grandma one day," it's almost like I was given permission to hope and dream again.

Thriving after my experience with cancer would depend on my initiative. If I was to succumb to the gloom and doom, I might as well die already. But if I wanted to live my life to its full potential, I had to be intentional about it. Anyone can be a passenger, but to sit in the driver's seat and decide your path takes determination.

A passenger is simply along for the ride. You can't make mistakes as a passenger, but you can't get better at driving either. As the driver, you are in charge and are constantly making decisions on your way to your destination. If you were like me when you were learning to drive, you made some costly mistakes, but experience was a good teacher and you even learned how to make a three-point turn like a boss.

It was officially time for me to make a three-point turn in my *life*.

The first thing I needed to do was figure out why my body was attacking me with rogue panic attacks and why my mind couldn't rest. What was at the root of all of this? I just *knew* that if I could figure this out, I could start to move on from this dark cloud.

My first move forward was attending a survivors symposium, where doctors would share new advances and veteran survivors would share hope for new survivors and their caregivers. Despite my initial turnoff from the name, I recruited Bruce into attending with me, hoping that it would be a healing experience.

The first person I saw was Jacki. We had a big hug, and she gave me some pamphlets. Looking around, I saw a melting pot of people affected by brain cancer. Oddly enough, everyone seemed pretty unaffected, except for the one man with a bunch of electrodes attached to his head. I suspected they were keeping him from having seizures. I felt pretty lucky to be among this group of strong people, until the next presenter walked up.

I can't even tell you what he looked like, because my eyes were glued to his presentation slide. He had case studies with photos of his patients. One was a story about a teen boy who battled brain cancer. The doctor showed us information about his case along with photos of his life. The last photo he showed us was of him making it to his dream college, standing in his dorm, wearing his school colors proudly. Just as I was getting caught up in this amazing story of triumph, the doctor went on to tell us that while he was able to fight his brain cancer, he died shortly after that photo was taken, from the cancer spreading to other vital organs.

Wait, what?

Maybe I was supposed to notice that his brain cancer treatment worked, but all I noticed in the moment was that a determined young boy with a promising future had *died*.

Next slide.

Oh, this was a good one. It was a graph of mortality rates! The graph was segregated by tumor type, grade, age of patient, and whether or not the tumor was fully resected. Well, this just got specific. I looked for my own situation on the chart. The number I saw might as well have been a bear. Fight-or-flight kicked in again, and I found myself in the middle of another panic attack.

I sank deep into my chair and into myself until he was done talking. Then I darted for the bathroom, falling into an empty stall with tears rolling down my face. "Ten years? Maybe?" The chart had said I had a one-in-three chance of surviving ten years. That was *not* long enough to raise my kids! That was not fifty-two years old! *Why the hell did I come to this thing? I'm supposed to be taking steps forward, not backward!*

In that moment I let down my guard—the new one I had just built on my road to overcoming the doom and gloom. I let myself fall apart all over again, right there in the bathroom stall. *What's the point? Why am I even alive? Is my life worth anything at all in the grand scheme of things?*

I was completely lost. But you know what's funny about being completely lost? You are completely in the moment. Looking forward or backward makes no sense, so you just sit in the moment. Realizing this for myself, I noticed my chest rising and falling. *I'm breathing.* I was indeed alive, and even if I didn't know why, I still had to do my part right now. My part was to keep it together. God's part was to keep me alive.

So I made a choice to unlock the stall, wipe my face, look in the mirror, and smile. It was a genuine smile that surprised me when I saw it. The knot in my stomach loosened, and the pain in my heart lost some of its sting. I'm telling you, smiling is a clever trick you can play on an upset body.

When I walked out of the bathroom, Bruce was waiting for me. He was curious about what I was feeling, but I couldn't talk about it yet without crying again, so I promised we'd talk after the symposium.

With his hand in mine, we walked back to the presentation room, and I flipped through one of the pamphlets Jacki had given me. One page in particular stood out. It was a large picture of a smiling middle-aged woman who gave a testimony that said, "Brain cancer was a blessing."

Never mind that she was talking about a mindset shift that positively affected her life. I wasn't there yet in my healing. In an instant my contentedness was replaced with rage. Just like that. I'm telling you, I was out of my mind! So many ups and downs. Maybe if I were a little less dramatic, healing would be a little easier. But honestly, was I the only one disturbed by all of this? Looking around at everyone else, who seemingly had their brain cancer situations figured out, I wondered how they could sit in their seats so calm, cool, and collected. Had they all just accepted their fates as previously graphed out? *Is it just me, or is this a completely demented way to live? I don't know how I'm going to get where they seem to be.*

When we left, Bruce waited for me to speak first.

"Ten years is not enough time to raise our kids."

He replied, "I know."

We walked in silence to our car, and when I closed the door I just started spilling all my thoughts and fears onto him. He was in the driver's seat. I needed to be in the passenger seat for a minute.

He knew what I needed. So he listened, made sure to throw in some encouraging words if I ever paused, and drove me straight to Windsor, one of my favorite restaurants in the area. When we arrived, my eyes were hugely puffy, but the deviled-egg dip with gorgonzola cheese and homemade potato chips brought me back to reality: the reality that these chips were seriously delicious, the reality that my husband was the strongest, most caring person on this earth, and the reality that I was lucky enough to have his kids. Everything I was grateful for started bubbling up to the top of my heart.

It's all right here. I already have everything I could ever need or want. I had love. *Love is the destination, and I'm already here.* By the end of that meal I was feeling miraculously content (again) and full.

A text I had previously sent off to Julia about the ten-years stat was met with her usual matter-of-fact, loving disposition: "Andy, that stat does not belong to you. You are an individual doing individual things that make a difference in the big picture. Don't you dare live by stupid stats." I liked that perspective.

Instead of buying into statistics, I made the choice to have faith. Even when all the signs pointed to an early grave, I had to choose to live over and over again. But even though I was *choosing* life—no matter how hard I fought for that mindset—I just didn't believe in my heart that I would live very long. Sometimes I didn't even believe that God, the Holy Spirit that walked with me through every other storm, would see me through *this* one. I got to a point in my faith where I thought that my own life was insignificant and that life in general was just a cruel game.

For the sake of my mental and physical health, I had to keep choosing faith. I needed to let God do His work and get out of the way. Looking back on my life, I could see that even the hardest parts gave way to the best parts. If God never allowed me to walk through hell, I would only be weaker for it. But all the hard parts gave me an edge, just like this could, if I let it.

I had to stop doubting God's plan so I could stop worrying. I had to choose to believe that what I had gone through and what I was currently going through were going to equip me for a better future.

I was drawing another line in the sand, and I needed my Heavenly Father to meet me there. The last time I did this, my earthly father had failed. Would God? This was it for me. If He didn't show up, I wasn't going over to His side. I wasn't asking anymore. I wasn't a passenger anymore. This wasn't a meek request. It was a declaration.

Because I had become so anguished in my faith, I asked Bruce, ever steady in his, to join me in the boldest prayer we'd ever prayed. We held hands, sitting in the middle of our bed, declaring my intention to live and our deep desire for God's *good* plan for my life—for all our lives. I was *declaring* my healing from the inside and out. We knew He was capable. Maybe He had already handed over my healing, and I just hadn't taken it yet. Maybe I was asking too much. Maybe I was too impatient. But in that moment, I knew something big was happening.

If the universe is expanding at God's will, surely my life can. Surely He loves me if He brought me into existence. But because being a Christian is about a *relationship* with God, we needed to have it out like this. He needed to see my passion, just as I knew His.

15. MY POOR THERAPIST

Walking laps around the block in our neighborhood became part of my daily routine. The panic attacks had become excessive despite my efforts to reason them away. My mind and body were still in battle, and walking was the only way I knew how to calm them both. But the relief was only temporary. By the time I'd walk back into my house, the heaviness would settle back onto my heart. I tried to act the way I knew I should feel, but my body could no longer be tricked. Not at this level. To top it off, I was still only getting a couple hours of sleep, so my sense of reality and hope were skewed completely.

I honestly thought I would be able to push through the hard parts. If I could just withstand the storm, one day it would pass on by. Or so I'd been hoping. Reality was that I'd been holding on for dear life, and nothing was changing.

On multiple occasions, my mom suggested I see a therapist or find a support group. Then Bruce started bringing it up. It's funny how moms just wiggle their way into our business, isn't it? I knew she was just trying to help, but if Bruce (the man who can see a mangled dead person the same morning he comes home to eat a perfectly normal breakfast with his family) thought it was about time I got help, I decided to take the idea more seriously. Just as my mom knew I would.

I remembered Jacki had once brought up therapy, too, but even still, I fought the idea. My head was a real mess, and I didn't want a therapist poking around in there, finding more things for me to deal with. I could barely deal with what I had going on now, never mind going back to my childhood to try and figure out the root of my crazy. I also didn't want to go to a support group and take on all the problems of everyone else, since my anxiety had made me an emotional sponge.

One morning Bruce came home with a therapist recommendation from a friend at work. Apparently even tough firefighters need to talk to someone sometimes. He handed me a scrap piece of paper with the name *Gail* written in chicken scratch above an email address and phone number. I was too nervous to call, not knowing if I'd get the front desk or a direct line where I'd hear the actual voice of the actual person about to get bombarded with all my drama. I decided to play it safe and send an email. Her reply was kind, and she offered to give me one of her emergency spots so I could see her sooner than later. She seemed genuine, so I took the appointment.

When I met Gail, the first thing I noticed was her bubbly yet calm demeanor. When I sat down on her couch, she asked questions and listened with empathy. The first appointment was basically me talking and talking and crying and crying. I felt a sense of release but also felt like I had totally confirmed why I needed to be there. I knew it would be a process to dig deep if I kept coming.

I called Bruce before I even left the parking lot.

"I just cried to that poor woman for an hour. I don't know how she can sit there and listen to people like me all day long."

"Well, do you feel better?"

"I do, actually." And just like that, I realized I needed to keep showing up for Gail, for me.

The next appointment was also a lot of crying. Gail would ask me questions I had already pondered myself, but when I heard the things that were in my head come out of my mouth, it broke my heart.

I kept telling her that I was okay, that I could talk about it. My tears were a physical reaction to something I wasn't quite sure about yet. It was confusing to cry so much and have no control over it.

In one particular conversation, she laughed at my response to the question, "What do you think will come of all of this?"

Now, Gail is as sweet as they come. I actually wish she were part of my family so I could see her all the time. But she *laughed* at me!

"Do you realize what you just said?"

Stunned, I shook my head, "No."

Her response was promoted by the same confession I'd made to Bruce—that everything that was happening to me, to us, was meant for everyone else. That this experience was for their story, not mine, because my ending was so close. What *else* could come of it?

"Andy, you are making yourself the sacrificial lamb of your own life! How can it be *your* life if you don't live it?! God didn't bring you this far to do nothing with you."

Now, Gail knew she could talk gospel to me, even in this place of business, because I had spoken it first. So she didn't hold back.

"For goodness sake, Andy! You are not a sacrificial lamb. You are not Jesus! Your life is *yours*."

I didn't know if I believed her—well, the Jesus part I knew, but my life being my own? That hadn't really sunk in before.

My "why" was my family and our future. I'd do anything for them, even go to therapy. I always put myself last, even in my own story apparently. You see, part of my issues around this include having an ingrained feeling of guilt. Remember when I apologized to Bruce for having cancer when we found out? Not only did I feel bad for possibly leaving my family too early, but, looking back on my life and even in the present, I didn't feel adequate to create the legacy I had hoped for.

Eventually Gail told me, "Don't spiral in all the things that you didn't do right along the way. That helps no one and takes away from your life *now*. A guilty mentality is like a debilitating prison, separating you and your gifts from the world. That is *not* what God wants for you. He wants you to grow. Circumstances might look like punishment for whatever is giving you a guilty conscience, but it's actually *discipline*. Don't get the two mixed. We all need discipline to do great things. Your maker wouldn't have woken you up today if he didn't have a reason to. You are here on purpose, and it is your duty to break this spiral and take your life back. Any adversity you are facing was put there to make you better than before. Any choice you are presented with is a chance to live a new life. Look forward, not backward, and watch the guilt fade away."

My "crazy" was starting to make sense, but a few sessions later, I still hadn't slept. I really wanted to talk about *that* today. I told her how my body had been physically fighting sleep. How I'd jerk myself awake as soon as I fell asleep, with a pounding heart and sometimes pouring sweat.

That Gail—she dropped a bomb on me like it was nothing.

"It's because you have PTSD."

One thing I was starting to learn about Gail was that she was very direct. I guess when you only have an hour a week to fix someone you have to get to the point. Again, I looked at her, stunned.

"But don't people with PTSD kill themselves?"

She laughed at me again. I didn't take it personally this time.

"No, you are an INFJ. You are seriously complex."

She was referring to my personality type again. And to not leave me hanging on the whole killing-myself fear, she quickly interrupted my thoughts with, "PTSD is something you *can* overcome. You are going to be okay."

Now that I was reassured I wasn't beyond help, I was becoming more interested in this whole *INFJ* term she kept using during our sessions. At my very first appointment I was given a questionnaire to take home and fill out. I remember completing it and looking at the results, thinking it was pretty interesting and accurate, but I hadn't really revisited it since. Now seemed like a good time to take a deeper look, since this wasn't the first time she had used my personality against my own theories.

Turns out, the INFJ personality is considered to be the world's rarest personality type, making up less than 2 percent of the entire world's population. INFJs are nicknamed "The Advocate" or "The Counselor" and have been described as "mysteri-ous," "intuitive," and "emotionally intelligent," yet often misunderstood. Basically, INFJs are weirdos. Here's how the popular site Truity.com explains it:

"The INFJ is an acronym used to describe one of the sixteen personality types created by Katharine Briggs and Isabel Myers. It stands for Introverted, iNtuitive, Feeling, Judging. INFJ indicates a person who is energized by time alone (Introverted), who focuses on ideas and concepts rather than facts and details (iNtuitive), who makes decisions based on feelings and values (Feeling) and who prefers to be planned and organized rather than spontaneous and flexible (Judging)."

And that just scratches the surface. There's a whole webpage that outlines me like I was carbon-printed from an INFJ blueprint. If you want to freak yourself out, take the personality test for yourself.

But if you do, it's important to remember that these personality types aren't set in stone. Just because you are wired one way doesn't mean you can't learn to grow in other ways. Over time your personality type might even change, as your experiences and circumstances change. Heck, the entire trajectory of your life can change if you work hard enough on yourself and your dreams.

A short-term dream of mine at the current moment in time was to finally go to Hawaii with Bruce for our ten-year anniversary. The date had been set and the trip had been booked, but I honestly wasn't sure I could make it on that plane, let alone endure a six-hour flight, with the way my anxiety had been snowballing. Gail and I talked through different techniques I could use to coach myself into getting through the plane ride without running up and down the center aisle screaming, "We're all going to die!"

I didn't want to get on that tiny plane with all the people, I didn't want to be strapped into my seat like a psych-ward patient, and I for sure didn't want to look out the window and see the distance between life and death if the pilot had a heart attack or the engine blew. With all of these irrational fears about death, I thought Gail was going to say I had mortality issues.

No, she told me I had *control* issues. Oh snap. I did. All this time I had been focusing on my *fears*, no matter how irrational, instead of *why* I was afraid. I was afraid because the reality of my mortality had made me realize I was not in control of everything. To stop being afraid, to stop worrying about my future, to overcome anxiety, I needed to overcome my control issues first. My homework was to write down everything I was afraid of and define *what* about losing control scared me. I had to get all of these swirling thoughts out of my head, onto paper, and face them. You know what? They weren't as scary on paper as they were in my head.

At my next session we talked about the progress I was making in realizing where my anxiety was stemming from, but we had yet to get to the root. To get to the root I had to talk about my past. *Great. The dreaded session where we get to talk about my childhood sexual abuse, and let's not forget the daddy issues.*

I get it. I had gone through more than a lot of people go through by the time I hit kindergarten. My mom and dad divorced when I was two, and my mom moved to Arizona to be close to family. My dad stayed in California to start a new family, and when I came to visit, it never felt like home. My dad and I had an okay relationship, but it's kind of hard to be close to someone you only see a couple times a year. When I did see him, I also saw some bad choices he made. He was always kind to me, but man, did he have a temper. At one point he wanted me to live with his new family, but being homesick whenever I flew out to see him was a pretty good indicator of where home was for me. Thankfully, after many meetings with lawyers and drawing pictures about whom I loved more, I was allowed to keep living with my mom. I didn't necessarily love her *more*, but I knew how to play the game, and I absolutely felt safer with her, even if she was a single mom like my dad pointed out every chance he got, as it was his only stance on why he should "get" me.

Somewhere around that time I was molested by my babysitter's son at the home daycare my mom would drop me off at while she worked. It was a regular occurrence, and the one time I overcame my fear of upsetting anyone and tried to tell my mom, it came out cryptic, and I quickly gave up on the conversation. Granted, I wasn't even in preschool yet, so my communication skills weren't great. Knowing I wasn't happy there, she enrolled me in a different, public daycare that was a much better experience. Later, in junior high, I mentioned it to my mom almost casually, as part of a conversation about someone else, but I had forgotten she didn't really know. She was enraged. I hated that it upset her like it did. That what was perfectly settled a moment ago had been disheveled to a tangled mess. She called other moms from the daycare days and found out that I wasn't the only one. She also found out that the teenager, who was now a man, had a daughter. When I learned that, I made up my mind that I *would* press charges. He needed to be formally found out for her sake. So I went along with all the meetings and psychology sessions to make the case. I remember I had the most amazing lawyer. He was a kind man, and I actually enjoyed our meetings. He knew we didn't have a lot of money, so he *had* to win, even if it was just my word against theirs.

On the morning of the deposition, he drove my mom and me to court in his fancy black car. I had never been in such a space contraption. Contemplating the intricate interior details of that car helped me regroup as I got ready to face the man who had taken more of me than he knew. Little ol' me—still a kid—was about to give it right back to him. I wouldn't waver. I needed to be strong and intentional with my words. Man, I hoped they'd come out right.

When I walked into the room, there was a big table with a lot of people in suits. The only ones not in suits were my old babysitter, her husband, and *him*. They didn't look well-to-do by any means. I could tell this case was financially devastating for their family. I had some compassion about that, but when they became defensive about what I believed they knew to be true, a fire started burning in my belly. I stared at him hard, but he never looked up. I was careful not to memorize his face, just to wait for his eyes to meet mine. But he was a coward, and he let his parents do all the talking. He just sat there, slumped in his chair. When it was my turn to talk I told the truth with conviction to all those strangers in suits. When I thought I was done, his lawyer, an adult man, asked me, almost embarrassingly, "But when it was happening, did it feel good?"

I was completely dumbstruck. I don't even think I'd had my first period yet, and this man was asking me about sexual pleasure? I had no idea what that meant. "No," I said with the best tween attitude I could muster. But the truth was, I was scared. This was a big deal, and it was all depending on me. The defense knew it and tried to break me.

His lawyer leaned in and asked me the same question again, this time with as much context as he could about what "feeling good" could mean.

"No, it did not feel good in any way."

I looked at the rest of the table, but no one was looking back at me. The defense lawyer was still leaning in toward me like he was about to probe again, but my lawyer did what everyone else in the room wanted to: he put his hand up and said, "That's enough. She said no."

I won the case, and the settlement money paid for my entire college tuition at Arizona State. When I left the courthouse that day, I was no longer a victim. I got to see my pain come full circle into something good. Not so much in the form of punishment of the abuser but in the form of grace—that this shell of a man was forced to face his demons and that his daughter might be spared from them. It was a victory in every sense.

The only hang-up was that when my dad got word that I had money, he came out of the woodwork to get his share. Another court date was set and would land on the day I was supposed to leave for high school cheer camp. Because I would miss the bus and my mom would be the one to drive me two hours up north after court, we packed the car with all my things, and I walked into the fancy downtown Phoenix courthouse in a big blue bow, a cheer shirt, Soffe shorts, and chunky white Nikes.

I was nervous to see my dad, but he didn't bother to fly in from California. My grandpa would represent him. There was no hug or hello. I wasn't his granddaughter that day; I was the competition. He wanted to win control of the money for his son. This time, I didn't get the small private room with the lawyers. I had to swear on the Bible and sit in the booth in front of strangers.

I answered all the questions that were asked of me and, at the end of the day, did not have to relinquish any of my settlement money or add my dad as a conservator to the account. Thankfully my mom was such a good conservator over the years that not only was I able to pay for college but I used the rest as a down payment on my first home with Bruce.

These were the major adversities I faced growing up. I know it could have been worse, but they were mine. They shaped me. I learned so much, and there were so many people who made me feel strong and safe along the way. I can look back on those hard times and see how God was working. How it all turned out for good.

But right now, I couldn't even pretend to see how this *brain cancer* was going to work out for good. To be completely transparent, I had never let go of my anger since seeing the young girl on life support in the room next to me. I had pushed things like this down, and therapy was pulling it all up.

Gail reminded me that God was still good, even if I was angry. That I was angry because I was afraid. That I was afraid because I wasn't in control.

The only thing I *was* in control of was my response to that fear and how that response would ultimately influence the future. I could choose a positive response of learning where this fear was rooted so I could pull it out, or I could choose to self-sabotage myself in the form of isolation and self-pity.

My kids were my motivation to choose the harder route, to keep showing up for my appointments with Gail and pick up every piece of my brokenness until I put a new version of myself together . . . a better version of myself.

Before cancer, I had truly thought I was living with purpose. In hindsight I could see that I had only been playing defense. On defense we react to the unpredictable in the moment we are experiencing it, with no forethought.

But living on purpose is playing offense. On offense, we set ourselves up for a more likely success by taking action on purpose toward what we want for our lives in response to real experiences. On offense, we can even manifest intentional moments instead of just reacting to them.

Realizing the distinction of how lopsided I'd been playing the game of life, I knew I wanted to *grow* through this. I needed to gain some offense skills. It was up to me to take back the life that fear had been controlling, and Gail was a great coach.

My next homework, or "practice assignment," was to write a note to myself. Not as myself, but as if I were my own mom. How would I encourage myself to keep going? What perspective would I choose?

This is what I wrote:

```
Fear is real, but it is deceitful.
It will morph and snowball until you
confuse it with the truth. Let it
go. Give your fears to God, and
trust He can handle anything. Trust
that He wants good for you and your
family. Trust that the best things
we get to experience are often the
result of struggle. Trust that your
```

> struggle is temporary. Trust that it
> will make you stronger and capable
> of handling the future. Trust God
> because . . . what's the risk of
> being wrong?

I did not edit my words. I just started writing, and that is exactly what came out. I was simply parenting myself, and it was exactly what I needed to hear. A very heavy weight was lifted off my heart that day as I chose to let go of my fears . . . over and over again.

I wasn't sure I'd talk about God in that letter since I was still so angry, but as I wrote, I realized I wasn't mad at God; I was mad at circumstances that scared me. I was so wrapped up in my anger that I forgot I could release my fears. I forgot that fear *isn't even real*. Fear is simply a response manufactured in our own minds to something we see or think about. It is *only* a reaction.

But God the Creator *is* real. All I had to do to know that was look back on my life to see His handiwork. If X hadn't happened, then Y wouldn't have either. My life was a perfect, intricate web of cause and effect, and I can tell you with certainty that if I had gotten everything I ever prayed for, I would have never experienced some of the greatest parts of my life. God would say "Not yet" when I thought I was ready or "Right now" when I didn't think I was. In both scenarios I could see now that my life was full of circumstances out of any person's foresight or control, and all of those purposeful circumstances had brought me to this very place in time.

After reflecting on my letter to myself, my anger subsided. As an act of resolution, I grabbed a yellow Post-it and wrote, *Stop being scared*, and placed it on my Bible. I used that Post-it as my bookmark and swore I wouldn't throw it away until fear could no longer grip me. It took me three years.

~~~

My capacity for work at Liquis and the gym was back, or close to one hundred percent. I was working odd hours at both, trying to figure out what felt best for my new intentional life that I had *still* been trying to pursue.

By chance, I was coaching the same class that Cidney showed up to take one afternoon. Afterward, we sat on the floor and talked a bit. It was all surface at first, and then, like almost every conversation with Cidney, it got real deep, real fast. I told her how I still felt a little crazy, like I was either on the outside watching my life like it was happening to someone else or I was way too far inside my own head. I also confessed that I was having a hard time with my identity after cancer, with people attaching labels to me like *survivor*, *epileptic*, and *PTSD sufferer*. I was all of these new things all of a sudden, and it didn't feel like the old me I had been chasing.

First she recommended I break my alcohol fast and drink a glass of wine to chill out, then she gave me some book recommendations. The first was

The Untethered Soul. The second was *The Alchemist.* But then after thinking about it for a second and taking into consideration how much I was overanalyzing everything, she told me to forget the first one and read *The Alchemist.* That night I hopped on Amazon and bought the book. Over the years, I've given a copy to about a dozen others. It was that good. It is both straightforward and full of perspective. The story and characters— they were all metaphors for people, places, or things in my life. It helped organize my chaos in a way that was entertaining and peaceful.

Meanwhile, therapy was getting much less painful and much more empowering. You can see the transformation happening in my journal entries:

```
5/16/16
Stop! Tell your thoughts to stop
when they go bad. Bring yourself
back to reality . . . to the pre-
sent moment. Try using humor in your
self-talk to keep things positive.

6/13/16
Give over, don't give up. My fears
are not attached to me. Find peace
and freedom in giving over instead
of holding on to an illusion of
control. Enjoy the ride more. Em-
brace the unexpected as an adventure
again.

10/3/16
A good fighter visualizes the win,
trains the mind as much as or more
than the body, learns from every
threat, eliminates negativity, is
steady and aware, is adaptable, but
not passive.
```

1/7/17
On harnessing anger . . . anger has a stigma that makes us feel like we should silence it. But anger isn't all bad. It motivates us. It makes us feel strong. It brings about change. It is powerful and should be handled with care but never silenced.

Next, Undated
NEW AGAIN. This perspective shift helps me stay positive and experience every day and everything as new—almost childlike. I *am not* in charge of what is *meant* to be. I *am* grateful for every *new* breath, *new* heartbeat, and *new* intelligent thought. Every day and every moment is a chance to be new.

That last one... that was the missing piece to my healing puzzle and the perspective that helped me move on from crying on Gail's couch.

This perspective was introduced to me in the middle of an ordinary Sunday sermon. Have you ever had one of those moments when you get a little freaked out because it feels like the pastor has been stalking you and wrote the message so that you specifically could hear it? Well, this was one of those moments. It felt even more divine because the pastor was my favorite of the group we have at Christ's Church of the Valley. I feel kind of bad having a favorite, but his intellect breaks through to me in ways I can't explain. Pastor Mark Moore said, "You are not your experiences." I perked up. Wait, what?

He then went on to say, "And all the labels we carry, those do not define us either." Then I'm sure he went on to say something about being children of God or something like that, but I don't know for sure, because everything around me went fuzzy.

Holy crap! *I am not my experiences.* How had I not realized this? We are so much more than our experiences. We are a work in progress. *Who I am is still in progress!* Cancer was not my identity. Epilepsy was not my identity. Depression was not my identity. Anxiety was not my identity. PTSD was not my identity. The INFJ personality type wasn't even my identity. When I finally realized this truth I actually *felt* new again—shedding the damage—baptized in his words.

16. EMBRACING MY NEW LIFE

Growth is necessary to thrive.

The upcoming flight to Hawaii was still looming. I made sure we had travel insurance just in case, but Bruce was adamant. "We're not going to use that. You're going to be fine."

I got the insurance anyway.

Bruce was—and still is—so steady and patient with me. But he is *not* easy on me. Never ever will he let me take the easy way out. I am grateful for a partner who holds me accountable when I am weak or when I don't know what I'm capable of. Remember that story about us running the track and climbing the bleachers? What I didn't mention about that time is that we would often go for hikes as well. Bruce would use my lack of direction to trick me into longer or harder routes when I wasn't even sure I could do the shorter one we'd set out to do. But I always felt empowered in the end, knowing I'd done more than I thought I could.

Besides helping me recover physically, he took every opportunity to find humor and make me laugh. He even worked extra hard to make me feel beautiful, and when my scar peeked out of my ponytail, he'd say I looked tough. Our marriage was truly better for this experience. If it had been the other way around and I were the caretaker, I'm not sure we'd have grown like we did. It wasn't always graceful, but it was imperfectly beautiful.

My heart was full, and I was grateful for that, even if I'd had to walk through hell to get here. It was the last thing I had expected to come out of this, honestly. I mean, you hope you'll be "stronger for it" like everyone says, but what does that even mean? What does that look like in real life? I was starting to see what it looked like for me. It was a deeper appreciation for what I already had, and that appreciation was motivation to thrive intentionally in life instead of continuing to live reactively.

Meanwhile, Julia was having her own moment of life's unexpected joys. I remember getting her text and looking at my phone, jaw dropped, with the words *So, I'm pregnant* on the screen. Even though we both knew she hadn't been planning for this, my first reaction was pure excitement. After all I'd been through, I knew God's biggest blessings came out of the unexpected. This was good. God is good.

~~~

As I was driving home from the gym one afternoon, Tim McGraw's "Live Like You Were Dying" came on the radio. I realize this is super corny. Are you imagining me driving, windows down, hair blowing in the wind, scar glowing in the sun, belting, "Someday I hope you get the chance, to live like you were dyyyyyyyyy-yinnnnnng . . . "?

I'm sad to disappoint, but that's not what happened at all. I was flipping through my radio presets when this song came on. I actually do like to sing in the car, but I wasn't in the mood for this song about cancer and death. As soon as I put my finger on the next preset button, that same corny lyric froze me: " . . . I hope you get the *chance* to live like you were dying."

The chance. I realized, from another perspective, that I was in a unique situation. That I *got* to face death, and I *get* to continually face it every six months. That is my *superpower*! Most people have no idea what it's like to have your life and your loved ones threatened by death. I do. It was hell on earth. It still is sometimes. But it didn't get me. It was my privilege to experience it and have *the chance* to turn it into something beautiful.

Like Bruce would say, we're all dying. What's important and what's not important is sometimes hard to decipher when you're in the thick of a busy and messy life, trying to live up to ridiculous expectations. Lucky for me, everything was clearly black and white now. What matters in life and what really doesn't. I finally understood what that lady in the pamphlet meant about her brain cancer being a blessing. It just took me longer to get there.

If you follow me on Instagram, you probably noticed I have a love for good quotes. Jules was the first to introduce me to motivational quotes and memes. I was hooked. Then again, I'm easy bait for all things sentimental. No more searching all the earmarks in my books or piles of notes for that one life-changing sentence—the internet was full of them! Some are painfully cheesy, some are shallow, but some are actually really good! I started collecting quotes in my phone, and then I found the Peptalk app. The app has a library of podcast-style motivational talks, but I particularly like the mashups. They're usually set to a theme, and various high-level coaches or leaders chime in with their words of wisdom. To make it extra motivating, it's set to triumphant music so you can visualize yourself as Rocky, punching the air, prepping for a fight. They get me so pumped! Here are a few quotes from one of these pep talks I found on a piece of paper shoved in my journal from the time I was processing everything. The theme of this particular podcast was "pain," delivered by Eric Thomas, PhD, and every word spoke to my soul.

> "You will never ever be successful until you turn your pain into greatness."

> "Allow your pain to push you from where you are to where you need to be."

> "Stop running from your pain and embrace it."

> "Your pain is going to be a part of your prize. Push yourself forward."

> "When you die, die on empty."

Processing my experience while seeking out motivation was helping me to open up my life. It opened my sense of gratitude, and it opened up my heart to chase opportunities. Failure was less scary in comparison to what I had already endured.

17. TRYING TO FLY

Courage is a better choice than comfort.

It was the moment of truth. Bruce and I were watching the planes arriving and departing through the big airport window.

It was sunrise and an absolutely beautiful sight. My carry-on was carefully packed with a book, headphones for the music and podcasts I'd downloaded, and a couple crossword puzzles my mom had gotten me. I don't think I'd done a crossword puzzle since grade school, but she thought it would help keep me distracted. Also in my bag was the rest of the clonazepam, left over from my emergency stash—just in case.

Back when we had traded this trip for a Best Western Hotel honeymoon, we swore we'd make it to Hawaii for our ten-year anniversary. Now here we were. We had planned and saved, and I had gone to therapy, for crying out loud. Making it on this plane was the biggest goal I had set for myself, and here I was closing in on the moment of truth. But who was I kidding? I was still a mess.

I honestly didn't know if I could trust myself to not have a total freak-out on the plane somewhere over the Pacific. On one hand, planes already bring back bad memories from my solo childhood flying experiences between Arizona and California to see my dad. On the other, I had made a lot of progress with my claustrophobia, thanks to all the scans. I had worked through all of this with Gail. I had a plan. *But six hours?* I was still iffy about the whole thing.

They called our boarding group. Bruce stood up to get in line. I did my best to turn off my brain and just go through the motions. *Stand in line. Take a step forward when the line moves. Stand again. Step again. Hand the flight attendant my ticket. Take my ticket back. Walk down the long hallway. Smile at the flight attendant inside the plane. Check out the captain's booth to make sure they look like responsible pilots.* I was officially *on* the plane.

It crossed my mind to turn around and run the other way. It really did. Seeing all those people on a mission to pack into that plane like sardines was overwhelming, but I chose to remain focused. My one and only goal was to find my seat. Row after row, we finally made it. Our seats were toward the back. I knew it might not be the smoothest flight, but we were close to the bathrooms—and an emergency exit.

Bruce gave me the aisle seat and took the middle. Keep in mind, he is over six feet tall and was folded up like a lawn chair while I was doing the thing where you put your foot in the aisle to stretch out. Refusing to buckle in just yet, I took a clonazepam and popped in my headphones.

It was another *Seinfeld* "Serenity now" moment. To evade the corresponding freak-out to the short-lived serenity-now tactic, I put another clonazepam under my tongue. "Please work fast," I prayed.

I had not had a drink of alcohol since my first brain surgery because I was afraid to feel altered or out of control, but clonazepam, I'll take it. I realize this is absurd, but it made perfect sense in the moment. As the plane sped up on the runway, I held Bruce's hand tight and closed my eyes. That moment when the plane disconnected from the earth was the moment I realized it was really happening. *We're going to Hawaii!* It was an equally exciting and terrifying thought.

I was trapped in that plane like I had been trapped in so many MRI machines before. This was better because I could move but worse because, timewise, it was like seven MRIs in a row. As I was contemplating this, the inflight movie started. *Okay, this* is *better. I can do this.*

I broke up the time with frequent trips to the farthest bathroom, as Gail and I had planned. Sooner than expected, we were descending and getting closer and closer to the water below us. I saw some shadows, and something—a dolphin, I guessed—broke the surface. We got so close to the ocean it was wild. At one point I thought we were going to glide straight onto the water, but in a split second the runway appeared, and we touched down on the island of Kauai. Everything was green. This desert girl was in awe. We had landed in paradise, or heaven—I couldn't decide.

Our friend Linda, who is a travel agent, planned the whole trip (and the travel insurance) and had arranged for us to be met with the most beautiful leis when we picked up our baggage at the all-outdoor airport. If there was ever a perfect climate, this was it. The air was cozy, not hot. The breeze was refreshing, not cold.

With flowers around our necks and permanent smiles on our faces we went to pick up our rental car, which would turn out to be a yellow convertible. Where else are you going to drive a bright-yellow convertible around and not feel completely ridiculous? Nowhere else. We were like little kids, giddy for a crazy convertible. In fact, getting to Hawaii had been a childhood dream of Bruce's. I'd heard the story told from his mom so many times about how he really wished they would build a bridge to Hawaii so he didn't have to fly when he was afraid of heights. Now here we were, about to drive off in a car looked like Bumblebee from *Transformers*.

With the top down, we drove through a magical tree tunnel on Maluhia Road on our way to Poipu Beach, where we'd be staying for the next week. The trees reached way up into the sky and touched branches at the top with only sparkles of sunshine peeking through. Everything seemed divine. Hair and flower leis blowing in the wind, reggae music on the radio, and love in our hearts. What a privilege to be in that moment.

The first thing we did when we got to our hotel was drop our bags, change into some comfy beach clothes, and walk down to touch the water. Just like our California tradition with Tavin and Grant. The sand was warm, not hot. The water was cool, not cold. Everywhere I looked, everything I felt, was perfection. We couldn't keep this all to ourselves, so we Facetimed my mom, who had the boys and showed them a glimpse of what we were experiencing. They were happy we had made it, but they were mostly happy that *we* were so happy. The kids wanted to be there so badly. We promised we'd come back with them someday, and I still can't wait for that day.

But right now, I was feeling real peace. The rest of the world seemed far away from the tiny island, and God seemed so close to me in this paradise He had created. I was grateful to experience it firsthand. We had really made it.

The first thing we did after checking in with our families was take a walk to explore the beach. Now I was the one in a childlike moment. Everything was new. I had never seen trees or plants like the ones here. I had never seen a pineapple grow nonchalantly in a flowerbed. I had no idea they even grew like that at all! I was so in awe that I made Bruce take part in my favorite childhood memory of lying down, head pressed against a tree trunk, looking up at the branches and leaves dancing. Never had I seen a tree dance like this one. He could only stand my silliness for so long before he stood up and put his hand out for mine and said, "Let's get a drink."

I kind of thought it would just be him getting a drink, but there was not a care in sight at the outdoor bar, not even mine. I thought this could be the moment I would break my fast and have the most Hawaiian drink they could make me. Before today, I had been afraid of alcohol. I didn't want to add poison into my body after it was so recently flooded with drugs for scans, surgeries, and pain. Then the whole getting-high experience had solidified that I wasn't about the mind-altered life. But for some reason, I felt safe in this little corner of the world. Safe enough to do something that scared me a little. Maybe it was the fresh-picked fruit in the drink, or maybe it was the realization that everything I was afraid of was not meant to be avoided but to be overcome.

Drinks in hand, we watched the sun sink into the water from lawn chairs placed in perfectly trimmed grass right off the sand. The sweetness on my tongue could not compare to the sweetness in my heart through that newly found perspective. *It didn't get me. I'm here today. Today is new—and so am I. I'm finally ready to* live.

The next day was our official ten-year anniversary. They say the highest risk for a marriage to fall apart is within the first ten years. We had somehow beaten those odds, even with our financial mess, living in a travel trailer for a year, and frickin' brain cancer. This day was not just another day; it was *amazing grace*. We failed a lot, independently and together. The difference maker was not luck or fairytale romance. It was that we both kept reaching for God whenever we fell. We were always reaching toward the same direction. Because of that we were pulled out of the fire over and over again. I think the odds are in favor of the ones who are the most relentless in this way. The ones who choose faith, the ones who choose hope, and mostly the ones who choose love. We had made it through ten years of marriage today, and we'd make it another ten years to beat my life-expectancy odds and then another ten years after that, to my very last scan. Anything is possible with that man next to me.

Over the next seven days we hiked the Nā Pali Coast and saw the most beautiful beaches and scenery you can't even imagine. We snorkeled in a tribal reef and learned about the traditions of Hawaiians from a young man with feet so calloused they may as well have been shoes. We saw dolphins jumping out of the water, so close to our boat we could touch them if we dared. But of all that we did and saw, one of my very favorite memories was on a lazy rainy day.

I mentioned before how the climate was perfection. Even a rainy day was no exception. The rain was not cold on our skin, and the dark clouds were merely shade. The wind was refreshing, and the warm air still held me like a hug. We stayed on the beach all day. When the rain came down harder we'd crawl into our oversized beach lounger and pull the hood down so all we could see was the sliver of space where the ocean and sky met. Cuddling, sleeping, and kissing, we only took breaks from our lounger—for garlic fries, blended mango mojitos, and a dip in the ocean— when the clouds did.

Our very last day was more exploring before our red-eye flight back to Arizona. In our yellow convertible we drove around Wailua Heritage Trail, looking for waterfalls and sea turtles. We had been hearing stories of how a sea-turtle sighting was a must on the island, because the locals believe they are good luck. We had snorkeled almost every day, with no luck finding a lucky turtle, but today, on our very last day, we saw *two* sea turtles! They were swimming together in the strong current next to a powerful blowhole in the rocks. There were so many people around us, all ecstatic at the turtle sighting, and the blowhole spews felt like nature was celebrating with us.

We officially did Hawaii right. Our pain ended in this place. I gave up my false sense of control over what would be next. I realized that there was no stopping what had been started, and the future would hold what it would. I found God in all the places I wasn't looking, and despite my faith wavering between unshakable and shattered, my solid ground was always found in the presence of my maker.

The truth isn't always easy to find, but it can always be seen working in the details. That is where I found my healing perspective. By looking at the hard parts from the hard angles, I was sprouting new life. It's easy to give up, but fighting to find the good is what fighting for your life looks like. It's not easy. But it's worth every growing pain when you can finally look back on all you've been though, better than before, better equipped for the big things to come.

Thirty-five thousand feet over the ocean, in the night sky, I was holding—not taking—my clonazepam this time. I surrendered to God over and over again as my racing heart started to settle, praying for Him to "catch me" if I fall for the rest of my life.

When the flight attendant passed by, I threw the pills away with my trash.

I had finally let go.

AFTERWORD

You could say that since Hawaii, we've been living messily ever after.

I'm still learning *not* to live six months at a time, between scans scheduled indefinitely into the future, but to just live. Most days I am at peace, but I still have my fair share of being human and letting my mind wander to worry about things I can't control.

I think what helps me overcome the worry more than anything is being in constant gratitude. For my life, for today, and for my loved ones. When we're all healthy, I'm thankful for that too.

I've come to understand that without this life-altering experience, I would not have an ever-present reminder of how fleeting life is. Nor would I have the hindsight to recognize the importance of living with intention.

It's safe to say that, before brain cancer, I was floating through life. I was thinking small. Now, when I find myself getting a little too comfortable, I remember that I am here on purpose, and to honor that, I should live that way too. On purpose.

Every single morning that I open my eyes I know in my heart and soul and mind and gut that God is not done with me yet. My story is not done. If you are reading this, neither is yours. In fact, both of our stories are intricately intertwined into the greatest story of all—God's story. The source of life and love wants to work out all of our pain for good, if we will just do our part.

My greatest hope is that as you've walked with me though my storm, you've also found peace as I have. I hope you know that no matter what you are going through, how detrimental it seems, how rocked to your core you've become, you can *always* be new again.

Hard experiences teach us to come out the other side reborn, better than before. For our trials, we are gifted a new perspective and the opportunity to live with intention toward a more fulfilling life than any of us could have ever imagined.

And those scars left behind? They are not a reminder of our damage but proof that we have overcome.

ACKNOWLEDGEMENTS

My husband, Bruce,
for seeing me as stronger than I am.

My sons, Tavin and Grant,
for being my motivation.

My mom, Jackie,
for nudging me to write and believing in me.

My stepdad and Liquis Digital co-founder, Brad,
for bringing my book-cover vision to life.

My pastor, Mark Moore, for delivering the sermon
that inspired the theme of this book.

My neurosurgeon, Dr. Nadar Sanai,
for his brilliance and determination
to do what others could not.

My friends and "characters" mentioned in this
book, for playing an important role in my healing.

My beta readers, who took the time to proofread my story, provide critical feedback, and give me the confidence to bare my soul.

Amanda Walker
Bruce Ptacek
Caitlin Oless
Cidney Wooten
Charlotte Shaff
Jackie Wolfe-Ball
Jaclyn Garcia
John Shaff
Julia Rice
Norma Ptacek
Rima Woo

ABOUT THE AUTHOR

Andy Leigh Ptacek is a wife and mom of two boys in sunny Arizona. While earning her BA in Journalism and Mass Communication from the Walter Cronkite School at Arizona State University, Andy became a Rocky Mountain Emmy nominee as an intern for the local ABC affiliate. She went on to co-found Liquis Digital, an online marketing agency, after her growing family brought her to realize that climbing the ladder at a nine-to-five wasn't her dream anymore. Nearly a decade and a thriving business later, Andy was diagnosed with inoperable brain cancer. Now she's sharing her powerful story with the perspective shifts that saved her sanity and her life so that others can know they, too, have the power to change their narrative.

CONNECT WITH ANDY

www.andythenewgirl.com

Instagram / Facebook / Twitter
@andythenewgirl

andy@andythenewgirl.com

53605845R00112

Made in the
USA
Lexington, KY